The Fire That Just Blinked Up

Stories from around the Family Table

Hope You Enjoy the Book 😊

Alan

To order additional copies of this book, contact:
Xlibris Corporation
1-888-795-4274
www.Xlibris.com
Orders@Xlibris.com
57828

ACKNOWLEDGEMENTS

I wish to thank our daughters, Alexis, Katie and Wendy, who provided the stimulus package for putting these stories on paper. The book allows a quick reference to the past which may somehow guide them in the future.

In memory of my mother, I am thankful for her interesting life which became the foundation and first story written in this book.

My siblings, who did not ask to be included in these stories, ended up in here anyway. I am proud of Jerry, Jim, Thom and Dede and note that they are pretty fair story tellers in their own right. Their input came from hours of family conversation following sweet tea and banana pudding.

Cheryl Hilderbrand coached me and provided many suggestions and the encouragement to simply keep writing it down. I believe Pat Trenton had fun assisting with a couple of the illustrations typified at the beginning of the chapters.

And, finally, thanks to my wife Lynda, who uplifted my spirit with her support and helped with the editing as well as her contributions on many of the illustrations. She encouraged the writing and the time necessary for the task. More importantly, through it all, she remains my best friend.

Contents

PREFACE

These stories are based on actual events. The details were provided from a memory of stories shared among family members, often derived from facts, but occasionally assisted by a little imagination. Relatives may recall segments of these stories from a different perspective and believe that their account may be more accurate. However, as a member of this family, I have had rocks thrown at me, a knife dropped onto my head, been awaked in the middle of the night as a joke, been tied up with rope in the role of Dale Evans so my older brothers could rescue me and shoot the bad cowboys, and been made to sit on a large wooden box for hours so the hog would not get away again. I am also the middle child, which explains a lot, and this gives me license to write these events as *I* remember them.

But none of that really matters because these stories are for our children and grandchildren who might, otherwise, never know of some of the things that fertilized the roots of their family tree. The book's title comes from one of the stories, but as each story was written, others "blinked up" as well. Some are still blinking up and have yet to be written, but I had to stop somewhere. These may not be great stories to be placed in the libraries of the world, but they may always find a place on the mantle in homes of the families tied to these tales by their heritage.

OUT IN THE COUNTRY

Can my urban grandchildren imagine growing up away from the city or crowded suburbs? It's more than just living in rural Georgia; it was living there in an age when technology was in its infancy. When we got a television, it had three channels and did not broadcast between midnight and 6:00 a.m. The phone had no dial, but did have a live operator who requested the number to be called, like MU 779, for example. The radio was a major source of communication for news, sports, and entertainment. The state patrol stretched a wire across the highway directly attached to a receiver to indicate the speed of each car as it passed by. If you were speeding, they radioed ahead to a roadblock where the driver was stopped and given a ticket. Letters were written by hand or on a manual typewriter.

There is no need for our children or grandchildren to return to those days, but it is pleasing to see a curious look on their faces as we tell about those times and watch as they try their best to discern life without a cell phone, satellite dish, or wireless laptop. Life without technological advances was not a "simple life" as some may believe. The days were filled with working, schooling, cooking, cleaning, gardening, and maintaining a shopping list when we went into town. We played outside when the work was completed. We learned very early about making beds, cutting the grass, keeping the yard clean, shelling peas, and pulling weeds. We did not have a large house or yard, but we were often told that what we did have would look clean inside and out. One basic rule was to do as you were told by adults because the consequences were equally basic and direct.

From the highway, there was a long gravel driveway leading up a hill to our house. It was a small five-room frame home covered with light grey asbestos siding and had a silvery tin roof and small porches on the front and the back. Mother did require a small indoor bathroom to be added before we moved in although there remained a clear path to an outhouse at the edge of the woods. As the family grew, our father framed and closed in the front and back porches to serve as bedrooms. A large pine tree stood near the house where a large tire hung by a rope, which served as our playground equipment. To the right of the house was a small barn for storage and canning and a workshop that later was used as a playroom that housed our own pinball machine that our father discovered and repaired.

As you turned from the highway into the drive, there was a white frame building on the left where our father operated the White Radio and TV repair shop. The shop was a 20' x 30' box that was large enough for a workbench, shelving for tubes and parts, a desk and file cabinet, an area to place TVs and radios brought in for repair, and just enough room remaining for a red Coca-Cola machine. Cokes were a nickel for a six-ounce bottle with the name of the manufacturing city on the bottom. More than once, I watched my oldest brother heat a nickel with one of the soldering irons then asked, "Would anyone like a nickel for a free coke?" It really doesn't take long to look at a hot nickel.

Dad had a large toolbox in his green carryall truck for the many tubes and parts required for the televisions of the 1950s. He made frequent house calls and was the only service technician on our side of the county. As he returned one afternoon from a call, he drove along an unpaved road around a curve and came to a narrow wooden bridge over Willow Creek. There in the middle of the bridge was a full-size police officer in a blue uniform with one hand raised, warning drivers to slow down. Dad stopped and soon realized the officer was a metal cutout, solidly bolted onto a large round metal base. With a Drink Coca-Cola sign in the other hand, the officer turned out to be one of the many portable school crosswalk guards located on streets all around the nation. Dad looked along the bridge and roadside, determined to find the prankster nearby, but no one was to be found. He then did the next best thing and loaded the big metal policeman into his truck and headed home. When he arrived, he rolled the heavy base through the front door and into the hall. Although he was unsure where the policeman would end up, he returned to his shop quite enlightened by his discovery.

All of us were outside when Mother returned home in the late afternoon that same day. She hurried into the house, seeking relief from a large glass of tea she drank before driving home from our grandmother's house in town. She quickly sat down in the bathroom without closing the door. With a sigh of relief, she turned to look into the hall where a large police officer stood staring back at her compromising position. She gave a loud cry and ran out of the house, just able to get her slacks up by the time she made it to the back door. We came to see what was causing the commotion and together went into the house to find the intruder. We could barely stop laughing long enough to tell Mother that it was the crosswalk guard Dad had brought home. We heard the crunching gravel with every step as Mother walked down the driveway to the shop and had a serious discussion about Dad's decision to put the sign in the hallway. She was clear in her explanation as to where the police officer would be slowing traffic in the future.

Other than the metal policeman and an occasional snake in the yard, Mother was not frightened very often. She approached raising the family in a practical manner and exhibited a resolve to provide her children with food, shelter, and clothing. She was a steadfast disciplinarian who directed each of us, at least once in our lives, to go outside and break our own switch. The swishing sound of a limber switch allowed us to remember our misbehavior through sound and feeling for better reinforcement. She never made idle threats when it came to redirecting our behavior.

Early one Saturday morning, she obviously had hoped to sleep just a while longer and called out to our bedroom, "If you boys don't get quiet, I'm going to come in there and gag all three of you!" Well, you might imagine with three boys ages five to eleven in a small bedroom, this statement caused immediate snickers, snorts, and giggles. True to her word, Mother walked in after a few minutes with three of our father's handkerchiefs. She swirled the handkerchiefs lengthwise into a roll, stood behind each one of us, and put the gag in our mouths, with each end securely tied into a knot. As she left, the message was clear: "Do not take those off if you know what's good for you." After the shock of actually being gagged, our laughter was muffled by the handkerchiefs and pillows because we did, in fact, know what was good for us. As breakfast time drew near, Mother later came in and removed each handkerchief and said nothing nor ever mentioned it again.

Our mother was also skilled in home remedies to treat most of our injuries and illnesses. When she determined that a dose of castor oil was required, she would provide us an orange slice to take the bitter taste out of our mouth. It really didn't help much, but it was a good idea. Stomach problems were no match for the enema treatment administered by lying on a towel right on the bathroom floor. The phrase "up yours" would probably never be used again by children today had they had the experience of that particular home remedy.

Congestion and a chest cold meant sleeping with Vicks VapoRub spread directly on your chest and under your nose to keep the passageways clear. Gargling with warm salty water may not be unusual, but not many children are familiar with also having a sore throat "mopped" with Mercurochrome on a cotton swab. A shot of bourbon mixed with honey and lemon made a great cough suppressant, especially in the middle of the night when Mother had to treat one of us when we were "coughing our heads off." Aspirin was about the strongest medicine we were given for fever. Our youngest brother, Thom, was about four years old when he ate several aspirin, even though he did not have a fever. When Mother discovered the opened bottle and had coaxed a confession out of the little guy, she began to administer glasses of warm salty water. Thom did not like it. Finally, it produced the intended result of vomiting several pieces of the aspirin and whatever else our four-year-old had consumed during the previous hours. By phone, the doctor recommended that we keep Thom awake for a few hours just to make sure he was not going to lapse into a coma. This was not easy to do for a child recovering from twelve glasses of salty water. We played games and walked down the driveway and back several times late into the night to keep him awake. After he finally was allowed to go to sleep, it was Mother who seemed to lapse into a coma after a long day of intense remedying.

We were not sick very often. Maybe it was due to all the vegetables we ate that came from our garden. Peas, beans, tomatoes, watermelon, peppers, cantaloupe, potatoes, and corn were grown in a half-acre garden next to the house. Our father would plow that area with a small walk-behind tractor. We thought the field seemed much bigger when it came time to pull weeds from around the plants. It was a frequent chore that lasted most of the summer. Shelling the peas and beans was another time-consuming job that we all shared. Each of us would be given a bowl with an amount selected by Mother, and we had to finish our portion before any playtime. We had to be on alert to make sure that one of the other brothers did not redistribute his share into another's bowl when they were not looking.

Our grandfather was running the tractor in the garden one afternoon when we noticed that he had stopped and was throwing rocks at something while yelling, "Bring me a hoe!" When he got the hoe, he chopped the head off a large black snake that was not being friendly toward our grandfather. My brother Jim and I were entertained by the wiggling and movement of the body, even though the snake's head was long gone. We soon had a grand idea of taking the snake over to the outhouse behind the home of two old maid sisters, and what fun it would be to put the squiggly, headless snake inside the door. We did exactly that and hid in the bushes to watch. Sure enough, within minutes, one of the elderly ladies walked down the path to their outhouse, opened the door, yelped, and ran as quickly as an old lady can back into the house. We took off and ran full speed back home, but it evidently was not fast enough. Mother had already been called. She preached, spanked, and threatened to "jerk a knot in our heads" if we ever did any thing like that again. We never really knew what that meant, but we were sure if there was any way to perform such a knot jerking, Mother could handle it.

There was ample opportunity among the boys growing up in the country to pull some sort of prank or to generally act foolish. We all participated in one way or another. When my oldest brother, Jerry, heard that I was going to write a few stories about our family, he immediately began to hope that I would not include the lawn mower story. He insists that it never happened, but I have a very clear memory of the all-star prank he engineered.

For several years, we cut the grass around our house with an electric mower. We had several extension cords connected so we could reach the outmost points of the yard. Each extension cord had one or more places repaired with black electrical tape, where we had gotten a little too close to the cord while the blade was whirling. Jerry was experienced enough to operate the mower without running over the cord too often. Just behind the plug where two cords were mated, there was a small area of exposed wire that had not been completely covered by the black tape. Jerry placed an empty five-gallon metal feed can on the wire in just the right place so the edge of the can pressed on the short section where there was bare wire. When he called me to come over and asked me to sit on the can, I hesitated because I was really unsure of his motives. He said, "It's nothing, I just want you to sit on the can." My memory here is certain. I compare it to having bumblebees in the back pockets of my blue jeans. The good news is that the shock was sufficient to have me vertically jump about four feet into the air, but the voltage was not strong enough to cause permanent brain damage. My rear end was only briefly numbed. I had no other experience by which to compare until I reached the tenth grade when Mr. Johnson from industrial arts gave me two licks with a paddle, which provided the exact same sensation, only lasting much longer. Jerry and Mr. Johnson both will deny being a party to any of this, but as it is often stated, "Truth is stranger than any fiction."

Growing up in the country may have had a lot to do with the choices we made in life. The idea of completing our chores before we play is one of life's lessons that can pave the way to success in relationships at home and work. Transferring that idea into the modern world of technology can be just as effective today as it was then.

COWETA AND MUSCOGEE

All school buses looked exactly alike. East Coweta School housed grades one through twelve. There was an aging two-story brick building for most classes, along with an additional smaller white frame structure on the right side that provided extra space for the first- and second-grade classrooms. Located behind the classroom buildings was a cafeteria building that provided space for meals and for assemblies or other special programs. As a first grader at the school in 1953, I attended class in the frame structure. A new school was under construction slated for opening the following school year. My main concern on the first day of school was to make sure that I could locate the right school bus in the afternoon so I would be able to get home.

My older brothers, Jerry and Jim, were school bus veterans and told me there was nothing to it. They said that our bus was the one parked right in front of the flagpole. Additionally, I should recognize our driver Mr. Snooks Lovett, who also ran a gas station and general store just down the highway from our house on State Route 16. But I worried about that bus all day on my first day of school. When we were finally dismissed at the end of the day, I walked out to the line of giant yellow buses; each one had parked facing the building. The smell of oil and gasoline permeated the air, and the sounds of children noisily boarding the buses added to the commotion of school dismissal. I clearly remember standing behind the flagpole looking out at a bus parked no more than four feet away. I leaned over with my hands on my knees and closed one eye to be sure that the bus was properly in line with the pole. It wasn't perfectly centered, but all I could see was the big FORD lettering across the hood and thought it had to be the bus parked in front of the flagpole. As I climbed aboard, Mr. Snooks was seated in the driver's seat. However, it was only after I saw Jim get on that I realized that there was, in fact, nothing to it.

The first-grade classroom had a white wooden box in the corner behind the teacher's desk. The box had a small arched doorway painted on the front and was surrounded by artificial flowers with a poster of a wildflower landscape taped on the wall. This was the beehive. Our teacher directed students to sit there when they needed time out from the other students, usually due to some unacceptable behavioral event. I'm not sure why I have such a vivid memory of the beehive, for we were only in school for several weeks before moving to Columbus, Georgia in Muscogee County. The move took us away from the beehive and from a ten-acre homesite in the country. The new place was a brick duplex house close enough to easily walk to school on a sidewalk.

At the new house, there were several different areas for kids to play—including school playgrounds, vacant lots, and about ten brick houses in the neighborhood that resembled old coastal forts damaged long ago by barrages of cannon attacks. The difference was that these houses had been severely damaged or destroyed by a tornado earlier in the year on April18, 1953. Some houses had only the walls remaining, providing a ready-made fort for young boys to climb and fight imaginary Indians.

Our duplex home rested on a hill with a level front yard, but on a downward slope all the way to the back of the property. This geographic feature resulted in a steep interior stairway between the two apartments leading outside at the back of the house. Here was the scene of a tumble on the stairs and which left me with a permanent scar when I bit almost all the way through my tongue. This was an unpleasant experience, but it allowed for a story supported by a visual aide each time I say "ahhh" in the doctor's office.

The incline left a lasting impression on several of us one day when we loaded into the Chevy Carryall. This truck/car was one of the first SUVs long before they bore a more modern-day label. Chevy designed a panel truck with windows and three rows of seats that were very much needed at the time for the four boys in our family. On this particular afternoon, we were waiting for our mother in the car parked along the side of the house, with Jim on the back row and Thom and I on the middle seat. Before Mother could get there, the vehicle began rolling slowly down the incline toward the backyard, steel clothesline pole, a neighbor's fence, and who knows what beyond that, dependent on our gradual increasing speed. The freewheeling may have been the result of our jostling around for the best seats, aided by the truck being out of gear. Whatever the reason, there was an immediate response by three kids, yelling some combination of "Whoa," or "Look out," and "Help!" All these sounds were generally mixed together at the same time. I recall leaning over the front seat, grabbing the steering wheel and pulling back as best I could. This may have been a commendable reaction for a first grader but was of little consequence in slowing the truck. Then, somehow, Jim simply appeared in the front seat and slid under the wheel and pushed the brake pedal, bringing us to a stop. He had advanced himself from the back row to the front seat in a single flying motion to rescue us and possibly save the wooden fence in the back. I suppose as a ten year old he had seen enough driving demonstrations to understand starting and stopping a full-size early SUV. But for us, the very brief out-of-control experience was as exciting as an Indiana Jones action scene.

While living in the duplex, Jerry contracted mumps. His cheeks and jaw were so swollen that he resembled the original round-faced comics character Charlie Brown. Having mumps usually meant that a child was out of school for at least three days. At the height of his fat-face ordeal, our dad brought home a milkshake and two comic books for Jerry. I remember thinking how I wished I had a milkshake and two comic books. And of course, you have to be careful for what you wish. Jim was next with the fat cheeks and milkshake, closely followed by my turn, except that I only really had one fat cheek but still got the milkshake and two comic books. I think baby Thom missed out on the contagious fun altogether, which made our father glad, since he had bought more treats than he had originally planned when the swellings first began.

Once everyone recovered, my older brothers were assigned by Mother to teach me to ride a bicycle. They must have been skilled instructors, for I recall only once running headlong into the shrubbery in front of the house as they let go of the bike while running alongside and when I was left to balance on my own. At least they didn't guide me toward the back and down the hill where there awaited much more trouble than a couple of bushes.

In December of my first-grade year, as what happens too often in early elementary years, a kid in the lunch line said to another student, "Well, you know your parents are Santa Claus." I remember standing there overhearing the comment, thinking, *What?* I immediately knew it to be true and wanted to go home right then and ask Mother about it. As the day went on, I came to realize that I probably didn't need to ask, and it really would be to my benefit if I kept on believing. I still do.

As the school year drew to an end, so ended my dad's belief that the employment grass was greener in Columbus, Georgia. We moved back into the same house in the country in Coweta County. I think my folks must have been attracted to those Indian names like Muscogee and Coweta. I was surprised that one of us didn't end up with one of those Creek names like Opotheyoholo White or something. This move meant back to the school bus and a ten-mile ride rather than a ten-minute walk.

Those years back in the country were filled with several "Hey, watch this" moments from four boys who were in constant motion when playing outside. There were also four boys living directly across the highway from us who regularly joined in the yard activities. Sonny, Ronnie, and Donnie were regular fixtures in our yard and home. Willie, the baby, had not made it to the big boy area just yet, nor had our sister, Denette, who came into the family in 1956.

Jerry often led the way in demonstrating his skills as the oldest brother. For example, all of us were gathered in the front yard when Ronnie came out of his house and was eating a big biscuit. Jerry said, "Watch while I sail this rock right over Ronnie's head." We watched as the trajectory was slightly below the intended path and struck Ronnie squarely in the middle of his forehead. He did not begin his loud wailing until the blood from the cut on his head reached his biscuit. Jerry used our favorite expletive: "Oh, crap!" Each of us testified to our mothers that the incident was an accident, thanks to Jerry's preannouncement of his actual rock-throwing intention.

Jerry might not be solely responsible for the injury because wherever Ronnie went, he was prone to becoming some part of an accident. He was noted to have survived having his arm caught in a wringer-washing machine and having a BB gun discharge and lodge a tiny BB right in the small scar where Jerry had hit him with a rock; and while four of us were climbing a tall tree, Ronnie selected a rotten limb, and he fell almost thirty feet to the ground. We thought he was dead and told his mother so, but he only had the breath knocked out of him and a mild concussion.

Jim was always right in the middle of all the daring antics of our neighborhood. He thought he was a champion bicyclist after getting an

English bicycle for Christmas. The early versions of geared bikes had hand brakes and narrow tires. I got a big red bike that same year from Western Auto. While it was standard in every way, I was very excited about a new bike and had little interest in an English bike. We had a long gravel driveway that was a good place to gain speed going downhill toward the highway. Jim like to go as fast as he could and ride over a big pile of crushed gravel just off the end of the driveway. Our father had a dump truck load of crushed rock delivered to our house, and it provided a ready-made Evil Knievel ramp. What Jim did not know some weeks later was that Dad had used a lot of the crushed gravel to fill in potholes on the driveway. He shoveled the rock from the back side of the pile, so as you drove down the driveway, the pile still looked just the same. A group of us was outside one afternoon, and Jim yelled the famous "Watch this!" The slick English bike went flying down the drive and rode up the pile, but now there was no longer a back side. The front end dropped, and Jim and his English bike almost completed a 360-degree flip. Of course, "almost" is the operative word here. He survived with only cuts and scrapes, but it was one of our most entertaining events.

One of Jim's friends, Henry, came for a visit one afternoon and had several questions about the English bicycle. He had never heard of such a thing and wondered why the tires were so skinny. Jim suggested that he ride the bike and experience it for himself. He rode around the yard for a minute to get the feel of this new-fangled bike. He then started down the driveway and immediately began to pick up speed on the downhill trip. Evidently, he forgot about the hand brake instructions, for he began to pedal backward as fast as he could but with zero effect on slowing himself down. About three quarters of the way down, Henry was traveling at respectable racing-bike speed and began to yell "Whaaaaaa!" as he approached the end of the drive and State Route 16. As he crossed over the highway near the speed of sound, we were very lucky that the oncoming traffic missed him by a wide margin. The big ditch on the other side of the road had tall grass that slowed Henry and helped to soften his fall but did result in the separation of him from the bike by about twenty feet. He stood in a daze but amazingly had only a bloody elbow from the ordeal. I'm not sure he enjoyed his visit with us, for I never saw Henry again after that day.

During this time in our lives, our father continued to be self-employed in the radio- and television-repair business. He possibly was unconcerned about his four boys growing up in the country, but in his eyes, when number five was a sweet, precious little girl, he started wondering about the future of providing for a big family on a limited self-employed income. He again renewed his contacts with friends in Columbus, and on Thanksgiving Day in 1957, we loaded a large open-air truck with all our belongings and returned to the city. This time, Dad sold the place in the country, and we made a commitment to live in town. We moved into a small three-bedroom, one-bath house on Warm Springs Road. Our father went through several cycles of working for a company, then leaving and opening his own business, closing and going back to work for someone else. This cycle repeated itself several times. The change often meant a change in cash flow, and we moved into other houses around town three more times as well. In 1962, we finally settled into a predominantly military neighborhood on the Fort Benning side of Columbus, and Dad finally settled into TV-repair job with a local company in town.

Columbus became our hometown. All five of us had our first jobs, first serious teenage loves, first cars, and earned high school diplomas while we lived in there. It seemed as if the country life easily drifted into our past and no longer played a part in who we were or who we later to become. But I discovered as I thought back to those times and tales, the active relationships with friends and family while we lived away from the city provided us a solid foundation for dealing with life.

FIRE STARTERS

During the early 1950s, there were many television programs and frequent movies that depicted the old West. We watched the likes of Roy Rogers, Gene Autry, Kit Carson, and John Wayne tame the unrest by chasing bad guys, saving pretty women from the proverbial lumber mill saw, and firing big guns at Indians who carried small bows and arrows. Many of these good deeds were done by a hero dressed in clean, star-studded shirt while riding a horse at full gallop. The .45-caliber handguns made a lot of noise but did not make holes in people when they were shot nor did the bullets cause blood to spurt all over the place. We had to wait about twenty-five years for Clint Eastwood to change all that by adding the realism of how the West was really won in the trendsetting movie *A Fist Full of Dollars.*

The early Hollywood version of settling the West had an impact on our family as we grew up during those years. The things we saw, we simply accepted. I can recall sitting on the floor watching one of those old Westerns on television one afternoon consumed by the usual riding, fighting, and shooting. I even had my own six-shooter and holster. Of course, it was a cap pistol. It only made noise as the hammer hit small amounts of powder contained in a tiny spot on a narrow roll of red paper. The paper advanced upward each time you fired the gun. Just about every boy I knew had a similar cap gun, and each one of us would have been sent to juvenile detention for making terroristic threats had we brought those toys to school in today's environment.

My three-year-old brother, Thom, was also watching the cowboys on TV that day, and he picked up my six-gun, walked up behind me, and whacked me right in the back of the head, just as he had seen the sheriff do to the bad guy. But unlike on TV, a metal cap gun can make quite a gash on the scalp, and the red stuff on my head was not ketchup. Mother stepped in before I could return the favor and choke my little brother. She took the gun, stopped the bleeding, and separated us before any further damage could be done. My guess is that the old West was really won more often through the common sense of mothers than from violence.

Not too long after that day, I asked Mother if I could go over to play at my friend David's house. She told me to stay home and to go outside and play in our yard. We lived in the country, and there were ample places to occupy most eight-year-olds. Our house sat back from the highway, and there was a large two- or three-acre sagebrush field between the house and my dad's shop near the road. David lived down the road two houses, but several hundred yards away. I decided that since Mother had narrowed my playing options, I would send him smoke signals so he would know I could not come over.

I remember thinking that this was a good plan because I had seen the TV Indians many times send smoke signals, warning that the cavalry was nearby or a herd of buffalo was headed toward the hunting party or that there would be a tribal meeting at sunset in the chief's teepee. All I had to do was to send a series of little puffs into the air necessary to get my message across. The plan seemed so good that I never considered that David could not read smoke signals nor did I know how to send them even if I had a copy of the smoke signal codebook. I determined that David could figure it out if I could get the smoke to rise over the fields. I mobilized my plan by first finding matches. Not just any match, but a box of big stick matches that Mother kept in the kitchen to light the stove. I wasn't sure that the sandpaper strip along the side of the box would work, so I picked up a brick to have the proper surface to strike the big matches when the time came. And finally, what to do about the authentic Indian blanket? I didn't have one, and something about this plan made me decide not to ask my mother for a blanket. I did find a large piece of cardboard in the barn and determined that it would serve my purpose well.

With materials in hand, I set out to find the right place to send smoke signals. It had to be in front in the field between the house and shop so David could clearly see the smoke from his front yard. I chose a spot several feet into the sage grass so I would have ready fuel to break off strands of the high grass and add to the fire. I placed a small pile of sagebrush on the ground and added several dead sticks from a nearby pine tree. Since the big stick matches would burn several seconds, it only took one match to get the fire going pretty well. I then took the cardboard and placed it over the fire and began to hold it down, move it off, hold it down, move it off, etc. There seemed to be more of a steady stream of smoke upward rather than the TV version of sending a message via little puffs.

Soon the cardboard blanket was also burning, along with my plan and my confidence. The smoke caused me to cough, and the only other sound was that of the sage and dry sticks crackling as they roasted. I decided that David had seen enough, and I began to stomp out the flames, but they had now moved away from the original pile with the sticks, and I noticed that the fire was moving out into the sagebrush at a rate well beyond a little boy's stomping ability. I had earlier seen Mother go down to my dad's shop near the highway, and since I was in a near-panic mode, I raced down to the shop, burst through the door, and proclaimed, "Mom, Dad, a fire just blinked up!"

My father wanted to know if the fire was behind the shed near the trash pile. I said, "No, it's in the front yard." My folks hurried up the hill to get rakes and shovels to fight the fire. I raced to my room and got under the bed, believing it was a safe haven. It was not. Even if I could not be seen, the smoke had produced a distinct odor of burnt pine and grass. The fire was extinguished before it burned too close to a wooded area that would have created flames even beyond an adult's stomping ability. Mother always seemed to enjoy telling that story because of my "it just blinked up" statement. It was a long time before I found out that the Indians used a wet blanket to lay over smoldering coals for the desired effect. I'm quite sure, however, that surviving American Indians would be proud that I had at least tried to preserve that piece of their culture.

When there is any type of fire event, almost everyone remembers one or two additional stories. Our neighbors lived across the highway and owned a lumber mill a couple of miles away from our house. On at least two occasions, I can remember my dad going to help our neighbor when fire broke out at the mill. We could look out across the highway and see an eerie glow above the trees providing illumination where there usually was no light. Sometimes, it could be controlled and only burn in the sawdust pile or the nearby stacks of timber. Another time, the fire damaged the shop and some equipment. Finally, there was a mill fire that burned completely out of control and permanently put an end to our neighbor's lumber business.

Our neighbors had four boys who were about the same age as the kids in our family. We spent a lot of time back and forth across the highway playing, eating, hanging around, and riding bikes. The adults spent a lot of time together playing Canasta and sipping a few drinks while trying to add a little fun in their lives as hardworking rural Georgians. It was during one of those card games when the adults came up with the idea of buying a lot in Florida about five or six hours away and building a small house as close to the beach as they could afford. The lot turned out to be about two miles from the beach, but close enough for a bunch of rambunctious country boys to swim and play in Florida. We built our place with one large room across the front serving as kitchen, dining room, and den. It had two small bedrooms in the back with a small bathroom squeezed in between. There was a screened porch on the side with those narrow overlapping windows that had to be cranked by hand to get them open or close. What more could we ask for? In addition to the beach, there were many times when we went to a roadside amusement park for the arcade games and rides. We drove down to the house during all seasons of the year, at all times of the day or night, usually staying a couple of days or as much as a week.

Our lot was one of the first to have a house built in the soon-to-be large subdivision. The subdivision streets were cut through sandy soil with a lot of undergrowth and tall Florida pine trees. When we built, there were only six houses in the entire subdivision, giving us freedom to roam the streets winding through the area. We also discovered several sandy trails that ran for miles all through the woods. We heard that this large wooded area was owned by the St. Joe Paper Company, which treated the pine trees as a crop and regularly harvested the resource.

It seemed that anyone could buy fireworks in Florida. Every ocean-view house or condo was treated to free entertainment almost every evening because somebody was shooting fireworks on the beach. Even in Florida, selling fireworks to minors was illegal, but the law had little to do with the reality of curious children with easy access to firecrackers, sparklers, and matches. During a trip to the beach in the fall of the year, the four boys in our family teamed up with three of our cousins and bought fireworks at a corner gas station near our house.

It was during adult nap time in the middle of the afternoon when we were sent out to play. We began to wander up the street to an area where there were no houses. There were a lot of firecrackers to light, and we wasted no time throwing them in the street and in the general direction of each other.

We then moved to putting them under cans, bottles, rocks, pinecones, or just about anything that could be tested to see how high an object could be blown into the sky. Next came lighting a string of firecrackers in an effort to produce a sound similar to a machine-gun firing. The older boys did the more daring things, the younger boys were delighted to join in as best we could, and the two youngest were instructed to watch. Our youngest brother, Thom, continued to complain until one of the older boys told him he could carry a book of matches, but no fireworks because he could get hurt.

We were having a grand old time when Thom walked up to the group and proudly announced, "I started my own fire." And as older brothers can do, we ignored him. After about the third attempt to share his success, we did happen to notice just off the side of the road, little brother had indeed started his own fire. More importantly, we discovered that the little fire was spreading in a circle that quickly burned through the dry underbrush. At first, the fire was only about ten to twelve feet in diameter, but there was a breeze directing our little brother's personal fire toward some taller underbrush and pine trees that reached as far as you could see into the forest.

We began throwing sand on the flames along the edge of the fire and were generally successful in the area near the road, but we were not having much luck on the back side of the circle in the direction of the blowing wind. One of the cousins, Tommy, was wearing a light jacket, and we told him to take it off so we could use it to beat out the flames. He grabbed and held tight on the collars of his jacket and informed us that we were not going to ruin his jacket by slapping it on any fire. So the sand throwing and stomping continued.

The four oldest boys were working downwind, but the flames were beginning to spread at about three times the rate of sand throwing. A call went out for me to go get the adults for help. I turned and ran back to the house as fast as I could. As I looked back over my shoulder, I did see my cousin now beating the fire for all he was worth with the jacket he had refused to give up earlier.

I don't believe there is anything quite as unnerving as having the dreaded word yelled to a group of three snoozing adults in the middle of their siesta. This was not the "it just blinked up" cry, for it had much more effect in a tone more along the lines of a "This is the *Titanic*, I think we just hit an iceberg" alarm. I explained the fireworks and quickly blamed out little brother for starting the fire. Our parents zoomed into action. They loaded brooms, rakes, and one shovel into the car, and we flew up the road.

In less than two minutes, Mother assessed the fire and gathered all seven boys and directed us to go to the house to wash the soot from our faces and hands. She then spun the tires, throwing gravel and making a loud screech as she drove away to make a call to the fire department. We did not have a telephone in the Florida house, and in 1959, cell phones were limited to Dick Tracy's watch depicted in the comic books. Mother located a neighbor's phone, and the U.S. Forestry Department responded quickly to the scene with trucks and tractors necessary to cut off the path of the fire. It took over two hours to contain and extinguish the blaze. Thom's fire had burned about twenty acres of St. Joe Paper Company land. The fire had generally consumed underbrush growth, but there were quite a few trees lost in the burned area. We were very lucky that no one was injured, and our only loss was my cousin's jacket, which had not performed very well as a fire extinguisher.

We stayed inside and played a lot rummy and checkers for the remainder of the day. That evening, our cousins and their mother loaded up their car and headed back home. The following morning, we walked over to visit two girls who were about our age and lived in one of the three houses on our street. We were sitting outside in the carport when a black sedan slowly drove by, stopped, backed up, and pulled into the driveway. Two men wearing dark suits with badges on their coat pocket walked up and asked to speak to the oldest boy in the group. Our oldest brother, Jerry, walked with them over near their car where they had a long conversation about the fire.

By this time, our youngest brother was curled in a frightened fetal position in a lawn chair mainly because when we saw badges, Jim and I jokingly said, "Uh-oh, looks like they are here to take away whoever started that fire." As it turned out, they didn't take away any of us away since we described what had happened as an accidental blaze and pleaded innocent to all charges. The officers were very clear about how the U.S. Forestry Department felt about kids, matches, and fireworks, but the firstborn took the brunt of the lecture. Our brother told us that the message was further emphasized by the obvious scarring on the hand and face of one of the Forestry investigators. They also had several questions about the location of the store that sold us the fireworks. We later heard that the only charges filed were those leveled at the store owner for selling fireworks to minors.

After that day, none of us ever shot fireworks again. OK, so that is a big lie, but we all remembered what had happened and were careful not to burn down someone else's woods.

HIGHER LEARNING

In July of 1946, two cousins founded Truett-McConnell College (TMC) in Cleveland, Georgia. It was a Christian-based, Baptist-supported institution and was an extension of a model private school operated by the men located over the mountain in Hiawassee, Georgia. None of the history of the school had anything to do with my choosing to go to TMC. My oldest brother, Jerry, went to college there, and it sounded like a really good place to go. It sounded even better since the school had little interest in a student's overall grade point average and SAT score. My high school counselor had advised me to go to a local technical school, but there was something about the idea of college I liked much better.

TMC has experienced somewhat of an identity problem. When Jerry attended in 1961, the school's athletic banner touted the teams as the "Mountaineers," which certainly seemed reasonable considering the geographic location in the mountains of north Georgia. When I arrived in 1965, there were new school colors, and they were recognized as the "Great Danes," with a 206-pound canine mascot to drive home the point. I think the new president at the time thought they could raise more money with a new logo and big dog. More recently, the school readopted the original school colors, and today, the teams are the mighty TMC "Bears," being indigenous to the rural mountainous region.

All the school's buildings currently are located on one campus less than two miles from town. The first year I attended the school, one of the boys' dormitory was located in town, housing about sixty students in an old military barracks. We moved into new dorms on campus the following year, which was a good thing considering the barracks were in a complete state of disrepair. The girls lived on campus and were under the careful watch of a strict dorm mother, with rules requiring a sign-in or sign-out system under a regimented curfew. The boys who lived in town came and went as they pleased, and few school officials actually came near the old dorm. In an effort to follow good health practices, most boys wore flip-flops as they stood on wooden slats in the open shower room to keep their feet from rotting off from the colorful growths along the wall and encircling the shower drain. There was an ever-present musty odor similar to the aroma found underneath two feet of dead leaves in an Amazon rain forest. Meanwhile, back on campus in the dining hall, the girls had to wear dresses, slacks, or long raincoats over their shorts to maintain the requirements of proper Baptist modesty.

On Fridays, many of the students packed and quickly left the campus for home. I did my best to find reasons to stay because the campus and mountains in the area provided a great opportunity to explore, meet new people, and create interesting things to do. I did not have car during my freshman year, so getting home was a major transportation event only worthy of extended holidays. What my roommate Lamar and I considered to be interesting was not nearly as interesting to school and community officials. We often would come up with ideas we thought as unique pranks and adventures. We never considered that some of our actions bordered on trespassing and/or misdemeanor.

In late October of our first year, a young professor new to the music department planned to travel back to his Illinois home to be married. He had only been in Georgia a short time and knew only a few staff members and even less of the students. We learned he lived in a house with a red door, just up the highway in Helen. That was all we really needed to know. During the week he left for his wedding, we began to collect all the old newspapers we could find. We drove to Helen and scouted around until we found a red door on a small home set back from the main highway. We looked in the window and verified by a diploma on the wall that it was the good professor's home. We then returned to campus until nightfall. Returning to the house that evening, we removed a screen and climbed through a window, opened a side door, and lugged all the stacks of newspaper inside. For the next three hours, we ripped and wadded newspaper until our hands and clothes were black with newsprint. We hung a cowbell in the bedsprings and literally filled the entire bedroom from floor to ceiling and wall to wall with large quantities of newspaper debris. We pushed the shreds of paper into the bedroom until we could close the door. Then we picked up any remaining evidence and even swept debris from the floor to make sure the couple would be unsuspecting of the intrusion when they returned from the blessed nuptial event.

Three weeks passed before we received feedback from our excursion. We had maintained the silence of the innocent, and the new professor really had no suspects and few friends to call for assistance. However, one day, while in his class, he made a side statement about all the newspapers to which we overeagerly replied, "Newspapers? What newspapers?" He stopped and did not move. Then without further comment, he continued class, but he now had his suspects. It all ended with a friendly discussion around Christmas, when we discovered that he and his new wife had indeed returned from the wedding on a Sunday evening after the long drive from Illinois. With his bride in his arms, he pulled open the bedroom door, and the true appreciation of our three hours of work provided a great surprise. He eventually climbed through all the paper to disassemble the bed and move it into another room. The story from his wife was that she burned newspaper in the fireplace for about two weeks. There was no comment about the bell.

Out in front of the house with the red door, Georgia State Route 75 connects the towns of Helen with Cleveland. Along the entire route between the two towns, you can admire Mount Yonah—the dominant landscape feature and one of the highest peaks in Georgia. Rising 3,143 feet, it can be seen for miles. The mountain features a large exposed granite cliff used regularly for training by U.S. Army Rangers and by rock-climbing enthusiasts. As students at nearby TMC, we hiked to the top and climbed down the rock face many times. The word *yonah* is the Cherokee word for "bear," as in "Go, TMC Bears!" Legend has it that the love between a Cherokee princess and a young warrior led to them jumping from the cliff rather than face being separated by their families. Being quite familiar with the cliff, I could only imagine that both lovers would have been immediately transported to a happy hunting ground.

Lamar and I were trying to earn extra money working one weekend painting in a newly constructed church addition, which was contracted by Lamar's father. Late in the day, the discussion turned to the boring nature of painting walls when we could be painting something much more challenging, such as Mount Yonah. We agreed that if we painted gigantic letters *TMC* on the rock cliff, it could be seen from the highway below. The project would honor the school and be a great challenge for dorm room 206. We began to make a list of materials, including paint, buckets, brushes, and rope. We chose bright yellow as the color for the letters and determined that we would need at least one gallon for each letter.

As we were returning to campus, we stopped at the large retailer Roses and purchased the least expensive items we could find from our list. Back on campus, there were two additional students who agreed to help with the project and a third enlisted to drive us to the mountain road at dusk and then to rendezvous at 2:00 a.m. to pick us up. There is a long, winding road up to the cliff two miles long. As we neared the top, we encountered a group of U.S. Army Rangers bivouacked for the weekend in mountain training. Two of us spoke to a couple of soldiers and told them we were camping on the mountain. During the conversation, the others moved the paint and buckets around the encampment away from the road. When we all made it to the top, we tied the ropes to a tree and climbed down the face of the cliff to chalk an outline for the first letter. We made the *T* about twenty-five feet high. The cliff has many handholds and footholds, so we believed that could do the work with the aid of a rope. It turned out that our two helpers really did not want to hang out on the cliff in the dark, leaving the actual artwork to Lamar and me.

We discovered that we could hold the rope and the handle of the paint bucket in one hand, paint with the other and hold steady the flashlight in an armpit or occasionally in our mouth. Painting in the dark on a mountainside cliff reduces the fear of heights since you cannot see the 100 to 150 feet down the rock face to the first tree line. The distance could best be comprehended when we finished a can of paint and dropped it off the cliff and heard it bounce and rattle for long time before it finally stopped. And speaking of empty cans, we made a quick revision to the project when we used all three gallons of bright yellow paint on the *T*. Running out of paint put an end to the evening's work, leaving us to pack up and walk back down and wait on a driver who overslept just a bit and picked us up around 3:30 a.m.

Of course, we were up at first light and drove out to see our handiwork. From the highway over two miles away, the yellow *T* was beautiful. At twenty-five feet high and about three feet wide, it turned out to be just the right size for the great cliff of Mount Yonah and could be easily seen by passing motorists below. We were so pleased that we soon began the next plan of attack.

Three weeks later, we returned with a third helper, seven gallons of paint, and extra rope. We determined to avoid interaction with the military altogether so our summit approach was modified. In the late afternoon, we were dropped off on an unpaved back road at the very base of the mountain under the cliffs. We began a direct assault climbing up the mountain without the convenience of the winding road. This was a new challenge, but we decided that if the Rangers were able to connect the giant *T* with our faces, we were toast. The resulting climb was rigorous, but we reached the top of the cliffs just before dark. Again, we fastened the ropes to pine trees along the cliff's edge and chalked off an equally giant *M*. Lamar and I again took care of most of the rope-clinging and painting.

Only near the end of our second trip did the first real thought of danger occur when we reached a point as we faced the uppermost point on the right side of the *M*. Our ropes were not quite long enough to swing out to an area where there were adequate footholds. In order to complete the bright yellow letter, Lamar painted the final section by holding the tip end of the rope in his left hand, paintbrush in the other, while I held and braced his left foot above my head from a small ledge below. There were a couple of factors leading to the end of the project. First, we ran out of paint, having depleted all seven gallons on the giant *M*. Second, to complete the *TMC* lettering, the cliff was much too uneven and treacherous, even for us.

As the evening ended, we walked back down the more traditional road to meet our ride. It turned out that the Army Rangers were not there on that particular weekend, so we would not have be imprisoned for defacing government property. Rumor has it that while trying to identify the culprits who had painted on their mountain, this very charge was noted in a letter from a military official to the president of Truett-McConnell College. The college president denied knowing anything about the incident, but we heard he was pleased to have the initials of the school displayed at over three thousand feet on the cliffs of Mount Yonah.

Our artistic team never took public credit nor even acknowledged playing any part in the bright yellow *TM*. We did delight in the accomplishment every time we drove on Highway 75 near the mountain. Thirty years later, my wife and I stood at the edge of the same cliff while I recapped the story for her. Lynda enthusiastically wanted to know, "What could you be thinking?" I'm sure I sounded like one of own our children when they were teenagers, and I could only reply, "It seemed like a good idea at the time."

There were several good ideas during those two years at junior college, and while we were chased into the woods by college staff late one night for rolling the dorm mother's car with toilet paper, we actually ended up in jail only once. The most difficult part about getting *into* jail was convincing the local sheriff to aid and abet by locking five of us in a cell and calling Mr. Johnson, our college choir director, to see if he really would come and bail us out. When the sheriff finally agreed, he really began to enjoy his part. He had us remove our personal items and take off our belts so we would not hang ourselves while in custody. He then took us to a large green metal door with white lettering announcing INSANE where he locked us up and left. He made the call to Mr. Johnson who initially denied knowing any of us. He did call back to the sheriff's office to confirm this was not a prank. He got dressed and came down and wrote a seventy-five-dollar check for our bail. We got a stern warning to get back to the dorm and to stay out of trouble. The sheriff waited several days before he destroyed the check and notified our bail bondsman that there were to be no charges filed. A few weeks later, one in our group, Ellis, "squealed" and told Mr. Johnson about the setup. For retaliation, we first considered cement shoes but settled on completely decorating his car at a wedding we all attended. Ellis was not the groom and drove home by himself with cans dragging and Just Married written all over his car.

We realize how lucky we were during our adventures. We explored abandoned copper mines in the area with no ropes and simple flashlights, climbed off trail to the bottom of Tallulah Gorge, climbed 153 feet to the top of Anna Ruby Falls, borrowed a parking meter from the city of Gainesville for a dorm-room decoration, and put a live possum in Clarence Arnold Skelton's room to see if he would notice. The good news is that after forty years, Lamar and I occasionally continue our explorations although we live on opposite sides of the country. We continue to share stories and have shared a few joint explorations in recent years.

I suppose the final direct TMC chapter closed in the spring of 1972. I was in my second year of teaching at Morrow High School with a bachelor's degree in sociology and about thirty-quarter hours toward a special education master's degree. The principal of the high school was Dale Turner. Mr. Turner was also a TMC alumnus and provided a colorful description of the school necessary to influence my older brother to go to TMC, which later had the same impact on me. I stopped by Mr. Turner's office one afternoon in early May to let him know that I was on my way to Cleveland for the TMC graduation ceremony. There were a couple of students from my former youth group who had completed their two years of study. Upon hearing this, Mr. Turner exclaimed, "Oh goodness, I have forgotten all about it! I'm president of the alumni association, and I'm supposed to be on the program. When you get there, please tell the college president that I am so sorry, but I cannot make it." I assured Mr. Turner that while I would arrive with little time to spare, I would try to let him know.

The traditional ceremony was held on the front lawn of the college arranged near a large water fountain and wrought iron gates. Graduates would march though the gates as a symbol of having completed course requirements. As we arrived, we met some friends and family of the students we knew and laughed about Mr. Turner forgetting about the graduation. We were handed a program as we selected our seats, and there listed as the third speaker was none other than Mr. Dale Turner. I excused myself and headed to the administration building where the processional was being staged. I found Dr. Fussell, president of the college, and shared with him the regrets from Mr. Turner. Without the slightest hesitation, he directed me over to a corner in his office where I would find a cap and gown, along with a master's degree-colored hood reserved for Mr. Turner. He simply said, "You can represent the alumni association, and there is no need to mention that Mr. Turner could not join us." I was placed second in line by an assistant, and we immediately began to process out of the building toward the fountain. As a large bell began to sound, the crowd stood and turned toward the officials, faculty, and students moving to the podium area. My family and friends were somewhat astounded to see me leading the way in full regalia. I could not wipe the sheepish grin from my face but tried to deliver the appropriate pomp and circumstance required for the occasion. We were seated on a raised platform facing the students and family.

Dr. Fussell stood and briefly welcomed distinguished guests, faculty, and parents. A minister came to the podium and welcomed Dr. Fussell, distinguished guests, faculty, and parents. As he began his prayer, the reality of what was supposed to happen next erased the grin from my face. I had to be twenty years younger than any of the others seated on the platform. Not a single speaker had long hair, a moustache, and wire-framed glasses. I thought, *Oh crap, what am I going to say?* As the minister pronounced "amen," I stood and went to the podium, and I began, "Dr. Fussell, distinguished quests, faculty, and students." To this day, the remainder of my speech is generally a blur. I recall mentioning the importance of the alumni association, the fond memories of my days at TMC, and the hope that they will always carry with them the things that provided a solid foundation for life. I did not mention that I was not Dale Turner. I sat down and continued to try and look as if I might be one of the distinguished guests. It was my hope that no one ever said, "Dale Turner was the worst speaker I ever heard." As I thought about that statement, the grin returned, for my name was never mentioned during the ceremony.

I hope all the Mountaineers, Great Danes, and Bears have fond memories from TMC upon which to build their lives. There may not be too many mountain-painting experiences, but several great learning opportunities just the same.

GOAT ROCK DAM

Jack and Joyce were among Mother's dearest friends. Mother and Joyce worked together at the local Sears, Roebuck and Co. store, and over the years, they worked in almost every department throughout the mall store. Joyce had a couple of children about the same age as Mother's two youngest, which resulted in a lot of conversations about work and family.

Jack and Joyce owned a trailer on one of the reservoir lakes between Georgia and Alabama. The trailer, on the Alabama side of the lake, was on a sloping lot that nestled down to a large cove. The trailer had a large screen porch that ran the length of the front, giving the house a rather permanent cabin effect. I had been there many times before it ever dawned on me that beneath the floor somewhere were wheels attached to the house. There was a dock for fishing along with a boathouse. The cove was a large area of quiet water ideal for swimming and fishing.

Children from both families learned to water-ski on the lake. There were many fish fries at the cabin—usually including fresh catfish, shellcracker, and crappie—dropped into a large kettle of hot grease and served with homemade hush puppies and slaw. I don't recall any complaints about how all that fried food couldn't be good for you, and had anyone actually thought about it, they must have kept it to themselves. Every time I think about the cabin at the backwater, there is a host of stories that come to mind.

The cabin was not a place a person would drive by on the way to another location. It was indeed one of those places that had to be a specific destination because if someone arrived at the cabin and didn't recognize the place, it meant they were one lost puppy. The place was located as were many homes built on one of the numerous fingers of land that jutted out into the lake, creating miles of uneven shoreline. The final four-mile stretch to Jack and Joyce's was along unpaved roads and required at least four turns before we got to the entrance, which really bore little resemblance to a driveway because it was often washed out and rutted.

When we finally arrived, we often had to wait until someone came out of the cabin to calm two dogs that assumed we were there to steal the house and the boat, and they did not want us to get out of the car. But once assured that we were just friendly fishermen, the dogs went back under the porch, and the canine greeting marked the beginning of a marvelous and peaceful break at the lake.

Swimming, fishing, and boating were a way of life once we found the cabin. Sometimes, we stayed overnight and discovered that taking a shower during our stay often proved to be more adventuresome than the normal bath routine at home. The shower stall was outside and consisted of four 2x4s with enough siding nailed between them to cover us from knee to neck. There was no light other than a single floodlight fastened to a corner of the trailer. The water was provided via a garden hose looped onto a hook in the stall. The corner light helped find the valve to turn on the water, but there was much left to the imagination in the dark stall. Also, the water was always delivered at a constant freeze-your-butt-off setting, which meant that you rarely ever had to wait your turn to take a shower since there was a brief period between beginning and end of each bath.

Life at the cabin became a routine way of life for Jack and Joyce, and they eventually replaced the trailer with a permanent small house with a comparably large screened front porch. They lived there for many years. We were pretty excited the first time we went to the new house at the lake and knew we now could have the comforts of air-conditioning and hot water. While the house did have those features, the new indoor shower looked as though it could have been rescued from a small sailboat and transferred into the bathroom. Since Jack was short and weighed about 260 pounds we not only wondered how he was able to take a shower, but also how could he get wet in the hard-to-reach places necessary to get clean. We decided not to ask and simply accepted the indoor hot shower as a great improvement.

The lake is a beautiful place for recreation and is part of a water and conservation system located behind Goat Rock Dam. The plant at the dam generates power and has been in operation since 1912. Much of the area around the dam is characterized by steep, rocky terrain, and the original contractors adopted one of many goats grazing in the area as a mascot during the construction and, hence, the naming of the dam. There are some less rocky areas bordering the lake designated for camping and picnics, and it has been an attraction for local families for years.

Our family went there when we were all kids, and my brother Jim quickly spied a small snake at the water's edge. Jim demonstrated his snake-catching skills and picked up this foot-long reptile from the bank. He was so proud and showed the critter to everyone. My father took a look and said that the snake needed to be thrown to the ground and that we should give it plenty of room because a water moccasin is poisonous, including the smaller ones. Jim's confident attitude changed abruptly, and he did exactly as he was told. The young snake handler became an accurate rock thrower, and the snake was soon in several smaller pieces and could no longer bite anyone. With that behind us, we continued to enjoy the area near Goat Rock Dam.

Lake Harding was formed behind the dam and is home to a variety of freshwater fish. We spent many hours fishing from the dock, along the shore, or in a boat out on the lake. There were several special moments when one of the kids caught their very first fish on the dock at the cabin. Many people believe there is too much work in the process of catching, cleaning, and cooking a fish. But when at the cabin, this process seemed to be a basic routine where everyone took part in getting the fish from the lake to the table. Sometimes, it was quite a learning process. The first time I tried to clean three catfish that we had caught, it seemed to occupy most of the day. A catfish has very sharp spiky fins on each side of the body and one pointing straight up just behind the head. It only takes one mistake to learn that avoiding those bad boys is an essential part of catfish cleaning. I grabbed the fish, hit it in the head, put my foot on his head to hold him down, used a knife and pliers, and begun to look for a chainsaw when my mother walked over to demonstrate the art of catfish cleaning. She put her hand over the top of the head while avoiding the top fin, placed her third finger and thumb, holding forward against the side fins, cut the skin all the way around behind the head, grabbed the loose skin with pliers, and simply pulled the entire skin right off. No hammer or chainsaw was required.

Mother had improved her fish-cleaning skills over the years and had become content to sit on the dock and catch crappie and bream, along with an occasional bass. She loved to use a lightweight rod and reel with a simple red-over-white plastic bob, using red worms or crickets for bait. She always brought crickets, and at the end of the day, she would hang the wire container inside the cabin to keep them cool and alive for the next morning's excursion. My brother Jerry and I were staying over one weekend, and after a long day of relaxing by the lake, we were really tired. As we lay there on the foldout sofa, he said that the noisy crickets were driving him crazy, and he didn't think he could get to sleep. Of course, I wanted to know, "What crickets?" It was one of those defining moments in my life when I realized that my hearing loss in the upper ranges had now moved into the significant loss range and that if I couldn't hear fifty crickets chirping, what else was I missing? Being a sensible adult concerned about my health, I waited about eight years before being fitted with hearing aids.

Mother was fishing with crickets one late afternoon, sitting on the dock, watching that little red-and-white cork float along. It is always fun to watch a cork, especially with freshwater fish, because sometimes the cork just sits and sits and, at times, seems to stare back. Other times, you may see it make a slight but quick jerk. This makes you think that a fish has brains enough just to nibble on the bait, but never really touching the hook for the specific purpose of frustrating the person fishing and generally making the worm pretty mad. But you really have to love it when that cork just disappears with a distinct "plop," and you know that something down there means business. That particular day, Mother experienced more of a dramatic "ka-bloop," and not only did the cork disappear, but the line also straightened out and the rod began to seriously bend over the edge of the dock. Mother responded, "Whoa! What have we got here?" She would reel in a little, and the fish would pull the line back out. Mother kept the tension on the lightweight line trying not to lose the fish. After several minutes, Mother was standing up and moving around the dock, trying to keep the fish from running under the dock while hoping that it would not break the line.

Mother thought she had a big bass on the line. Jack laughed and speculated that it was only an old carp and how she would be much better off simply cutting the line and saving her strength. Mother of course had her hands full and, at the time, was unable to throw a can of worms at Jack. She was now more determined than ever to prove a point. By this time, she had worked her way off the dock and down to the shore because she believed that her best bet was to keep the tension on the line and drag this guy out of the lake. Soon, she was knee-deep in the lake but not giving in, when finally she started making some progress on reeling in the fish. Both fish and Mother were getting tired, but this fish was about to meet a certain destiny, and it would not be able to brag to the other fish about how he was the one that got away.

On that day, Mother literally dragged from the lake a crappie weighing three pounds and eleven ounces. An average crappie is usually one pound or less, and the state record for a freshwater crappie is four pounds and four ounces. So this was big fish. It was a fish that was mounted and hung on Mother's wall for years to come. We know that Mother was proud of this special catch, but we always guessed that she spent the money for the taxidermist so that Jack would always be reminded of his comment, allowing Mother to have the last laugh.

THE SHALLOW END OF THE POOL

Shorter College in Rome, Georgia, presented a bachelor of arts degree to me in May of 1970. There were several areas of interest I had throughout the years of undergraduate school, including music, psychology, and sociology. The music experience was enlightening, but I did not have the talent to pursue a music career, except possibly for church music, which never really seemed to be a full-time vocational choice. My journey into the world of psychology was short-lived when the major professor at the college turned out to be an atheist and slam-dunked me on a required paper on "Why I Believe There Is a God." God may have enjoyed it, but Dr. Valenski was not impressed. I finally settled in with sociology because at the time, it offered the path of least resistance, and I could not afford to keep changing my major.

The requirements for a degree in sociology were met in midyear between semesters. So what now? The coursework possibly helped me to understand why some people behave as they do when in groups, but there was no one lined up at my door offering a job. I eventually put my name on a list with the local school system to work as a substitute teacher. When that happens, you have opportunities to stand in front of classrooms at all grade levels and receive a thimbleful of experience in classroom instruction, along with a bucketful of indoctrination in classroom discipline. Several students must have known how I had treated substitute teachers when I was in school because they found several ways to challenge me while I was in their classroom. However, it was a job that did not make me feel as if I were in a foreign country, but instead, there seemed to be a direct connection between my interest in working in church youth programs and working with children in the public school. In those days, we stood and pledged the flag and said the Lord's Prayer and often recited the Twenty-third Psalm, so there were some similarities.

The administrator for curriculum and instruction at the county's central office called and requested that I come to her office to discuss teaching in the school system. During our meeting, she asked if I wanted to teach in a new program starting the next school year called special education. Before I could really find out about this new program, she scheduled me to accompany her and another teacher to West Georgia College; I enrolled in the master's program, scheduled ten-quarter hours during the summer session, got a provisional teaching certificate in this new area, and began at Red Bud School by the end of August. As a result of just trying to be a nice guy, I had written checks, had a college ID badge, was driving eighty miles to campus four days a week, and had signed a contract to teach in the 1970-71 school year. At the time, it seemed like a good idea. Actually, it was the only idea where I could perform a service and someone give me money for the effort.

The classroom assignment included students in grades four through seven assigned to be with me all day. State regulations limited the class size to fifteen special students in one room. The program was not only new to me, but it was also new to the entire school. The fifteen children were selected by teachers' referral based on the performance and ability of the children. There was no comprehensive testing of individual children. As a result, teachers had a tendency to recommend those students who were so far behind other children academically that they might never be able to catch up. The state provided a label for this group as educable mentally retarded or EMR. At the time, we had not learned of the need to be socially sensitive to the brand of being a "retard," but were purposeful in trying to get these students down the education road, albeit in a different wagon.

With only fifteen children, the school principal Oldfield decided that we did not need a regular-sized classroom, so we were assigned the smaller room that once served as a cannery, located next to the boiler room. It was located beneath the auditorium stage and accessible only via steps leading down to an outside entrance. During the teacher-planning days before school began, I painted the walls of the classroom and commandeered desks and well-used textbooks from teachers who only shook their heads when they discovered I had Dustin, Jacob, and Bernice among the fabulous fifteen.

Parents of three of the students came by during the preplanning days to discuss their child's program with the new teacher. One mother brought extra clothes in case her daughter had one of her accidents during the day, another dropped off two large print books that her son liked to look at if we had free time, and the third parent spent much time explaining that his son's learning difficulties were a direct result from problems on his mother's side of the family. These three were not parents of the three children listed earlier by the head-shaking teachers.

When the daily schedule was distributed to the teachers, I learned the real meaning of a self-contained classroom: one teacher and fifteen children all day, every day. That would include one happy group for lunch, PE, art, music, and academics. I supposed that Principal Oldfield had not reviewed my transcript closely enough to see that I had ten-quarter hours in education beyond a degree in sociology. He did, however, want to make me feel a part of the team when the bus duty schedule was developed so that I might interact with staff and children every third week in the mornings and afternoons.

In the classroom, we developed our own schedule, posted it on the wall, and changed it whenever we decided we wanted to go play softball in the morning as opposed to the afternoon. Lunch period was the same each day because the lunchroom ladies, while great cooks, obviously were recovering air traffic controllers who insisted that each group fly in, land, and take off precisely on schedule. Other than lunch, our class generally was left on our own. The students stayed busy, the days came and went, and no school administrator ever came into our room. As long as lunch money was collected and the attendance register completed on time, in ink, we had smooth sailing. The assistant principal for the lower grades was especially grateful, for I never brought a student into his office for discipline. He had frequently seen many of our students the year before, and three of our boys had made his all-star paddling team.

Dustin was one of those students. He had been retained at least once, had very poor reading skills and a severe speech problem resulting in the absence of *S* sounds in his conversations. To Dustin, I was always "Micker White." He had been ridiculed for years until he became large and strong enough to beat anybody's butt who said anything to his face about his lack of verbal skills. There was no paddle in our room, so Dustin did many push-ups, sat in a desk next to the teacher's desk, and was subjected to several other disciplinary ordeals that are no longer accepted in today's positive behavioral approach classrooms. But we did learn to get along.

Dustin frequently talked about going fishing, with no *S* of course. It was during one of his discourses on the subject that we struck a deal. I agreed to take Dustin fishing if he could demonstrate improvement in his behavior during the month. He continued to be a rural Georgia boy who physically plowed his way through every social interaction in his life, but he worked hard at following directions in the classroom for the month. He kept his end of the bargain, and it became time for me to keep mine.

My friend Ray and I fished several times in a small lake a few miles from the school. He knew of the agreement I had with Dustin and arranged one afternoon to meet us at the lake. I had called Dustin's mother and set the time I would pick him up. His mother said, "Micker White, we thank you for taking him with you." It seemed that Dustin had been wading in the shallow end of the gene pool when it came to speech and language skills.

We discovered a lot that day from Dustin. He had only been fishing about twice in his life. He brought a small rod and reel, which was missing about four inches from the tip of the rod. He had never been in a boat and put his arms through the straps on the seat cushion looking as if he was wearing a parachute, and sat down in the very bottom of the boat, gripping the sides for all he was worth. When we got him on a boat seat, seated on the cushion, he began casting his line as if he were throwing rocks at a snake. Ray and I were each hit in the back of the head at least once by the lead weights on his line, and Dustin successfully hooked my shirtsleeve, barely missing the skin. Dustin did not catch a single fish. If I could have willed even a small bream to accidently end up on Dustin's hook, I surely would have done so. At the end of the day when we presented the fish to Dustin's mother, I simply said, "Here are the fish we caught." The story of who caught what was left up to Dustin. In school, Dustin was a challenge every day, but now we had a much better understanding of each other.

Another constant disciplinary challenge came from two sixth graders who were our largest boys, each weighing over 180 pounds and grossly out of shape. Donald was visually impaired, and Martin simply pestered everyone because he had never received positive feedback socially or academically. These two guys were a nonstop bumper car ride without the cars. Tugging, punching, pinching, and hitting characterized the routine exchange between the boys almost every day. I separated them, had them do extra work, counseled them about their behavior, but still no luck. One morning, they bumped and punched each other on the way to and from the pencil sharpener, a favorite place to get attention. It was then I had another idea that would have been unacceptable by the administration. I told them that when we went out for our recess, we were going to let them fight it out. They looked shocked, but neither could back down because of their ongoing feud.

We went outside after the other classes had returned to their rooms. I sat the other members of the class on a bank overlooking the ball field and told them there was to be no cheering or screaming for one or the other because we would disturb other classes. I took the boys down to a grassy area that I hoped would soften any fall. The rules were simple: "You may now fight it out when I say go! Fight fair and square with no scratching like a couple of girls. If at any time there is blood showing, the fight is over." I then stood back, prayed that this would not be my last day in teaching, and told them to have at it.

The fight began with some serious swings, then a headlock while wrestling to the ground; a few more punches while on the ground and Donald scrambled up with a small bleeding cut on his lip. Fight over. It must have lasted a good two full minutes. But now both boys were satisfied with the results: Martin could say he had won the fight, and Donald had a red badge of courage for his effort. I made them shake hands and told them that their fighting days were over, and to my amazement, they were. It was as if some unspoken truce had been issued between them to ensure there would not to be another heavyweight event again. The boys did continue much of their verbal crossfire, but it was controllable and did not disrupt the entire class.

Although our classroom was isolated, I tried to take part in some of the regular school activities. I helped the chorus teacher with a couple of soloists and the high school quartet. I raised my hand in faculty meetings when Principal Oldfield needed a volunteer. I joined the teacher's association. One of the great moments in special education history came during the regular afternoon announcements made by the principal. This particular meaningful informational proclamation listed those who could be contacted for the upcoming faculty-student basketball fund-raiser. The loud speaker blared, *"See Mr. Johnson in the math department if you can help with refreshments and check with Mr. White, our retarded teacher, for information about tickets."* So there it was. Both students and teacher now clearly knew our place in the school.

In 1970, there were traveling school psychologists who provided intellectual assessments of special needs students. Near the end of the first ten weeks of school, one of the state's school psychologists came to our system to formally assess each of the students in my class. School systems today have their own school psychologists on staff. They develop comprehensive individual educational plans and have extensive support services for special needs children. But we were just beginning, and Red Bud only had Micker White. The psychologist assessed all fifteen students over a period of two and one-half days. Interestingly enough, all but one student met some type of special needs criteria. About the worst thing we could have done was to send that single child back to a regular classroom. But that is what we did. I think we both cried that day because each of us knew that he was so far behind that he had little hope of success in the regular sixth grade.

When the final assessment list was posted for the fourteen children who officially made it into my classroom, we had a mix of mildly disabled children: two students were tested in the "trainable" level (now moderately disabled)—one visually impaired and one emotionally disturbed child. What a crew! There was no mystery surrounding the reasons for teachers to refer these children to a special program. Their presence in a regular classroom had always created some type of disruption to the larger group.

When it came to disruption, Bernice was a child in constant motion. She was the only minority student in the class and was a small, wiry-framed girl whose actions demanded attention from everyone in her vicinity. She could borrow a pencil, go to the pencil sharpener, ask someone about their shoes, look out the window, knock a book from someone's desk, and ask what time it was, all in a single fluid movement. She was always astonished by my request to return to her desk, and she insisted that she had done nothing wrong. Each of the individual actions was not a problem, but when linked together by Bernice, six students and her teacher would be interrupted in some way. She was happiest when she got attention. She began to stir a feeling of impatience in adults within about eight minutes of getting off the school bus.

My own ability to demonstrate patience with Bernice became much improved when I learned that her mother had passed away, and she lived with her father and an older brother, where both had dropped out of school. By October of the school year, Bernice had discovered my home phone number and was calling about two or three times a week. She usually called when she had been left alone when her father was working in the evenings. I would always talk with her and, for the most part, was successful in keeping the conversations brief. Once, while speaking with her, there was a loud *BANG!* I said, "Bernice, are you all right?" She replied, "I just hit the table with a stick 'cause that rat was trying to get my jelly sandwich."

Several times, I handed the phone to anyone who might be visiting and let them talk with Bernice. It really didn't matter because she would talk with anyone. At the end of the school year, I moved away to metro Atlanta and to another school system. About two months after the move, I received a call on a Sunday afternoon. I answered, and the operator said, "Little girl, is this the Mr. White you want?" Bernice had found me once again. It was long distance and the last time I spoke to her. About six years later while working at the Department of Education, a good friend who worked in that school district sent me a copy of Bernice's high school diploma. I should have framed it and hung it on my wall, for she taught me much more than I could have ever taught her. That first year remains my favorite in all of the thirty-seven years I spent in education.

THE LOVE BUG

Mother spent a substantial part of her life taking care of five children and, at the same time, trying to figure out what to do about our daddy. She took good care of the children and seemed to put up with his dependent behavior. Maybe she did what she had to do for the five of us, or possibly, she believed she had a limited number of choices. But she probably knew that after the youngest went away to school, she could return to work where she would become much less dependent on the traditional breadwinner. Most of the stories I recall about our mother highlight her independence. As you read this story, you may wonder why I bother to make special note of her self-reliance since Mother's actions usually stand alone in making the point.

Audrey Brunettie Cottle was born in February of 1923. I don't know why her parents chose to give her that name. Her mother was named Ara, and she possibly was trying to make up for the shortcomings of her own tiny name. But Mother was Audrey to most of her friends throughout her school years. She added the last name White when she married our father in 1941. We won't even begin to deal with his name and will leave it at DJ for the time being. I don't know why our daddy and several other close friends settled on calling her Brunettie, but they did. Most of her friends at work used the Audrey label, as did others later, when she was considered a senior citizen. Others made a miserable attempt at pronouncing her middle name, but Mother never corrected them and just went along with whatever came out.

But none of those given names mattered to us after 1943 with the arrival of the firstborn, DJ Junior. It was then that Audrey Brunettie Cottle White came to be known as Mother. The brood continued to expand in 1944, 1947, 1952, and, again, 1956, when the only girl was born after four boys in a row.

Mother's name went through another significant change in 1967 with the arrival of the first grandchild who was encouraged simply to call our mother Mema. My brother and his wife supported this shortened version of "grandmother" so that their son would never be traumatized by having to pronounce "Brunettie." And so it was from that time, including the day she passed away in 2004, Mother was known as and continues to be remembered as Mema.

We experienced several family crises affecting the development of our sibling relationships. Typically, family protocol requires that an older brother respond to his sister's telephone call of distress in a supportive, caring manner. I felt the support protocol quickly breaking down when my sister, Dede, called to say, *"I don't know what to do I'm sorry I called you but mother has cut the tires and kenny is here but she didn't know it I can't believe she did it what am I going to do can you help me?"*

This rapid-fire plea was delivered with electrifying passion over the course of a single breath. I could almost see her tears across the one hundred miles of phone lines that separated us.

During the next several minutes, Dede described the sequence of events involving her, her ex-husband (soon to be routinely referred to as D. A. Kenny), her red Volkswagen, and our mother, Mema. I told Dede that I would come to help and would get there as quickly as I could travel the one hundred miles. As I hung up, I could only wonder why my sister hadn't called our oldest brother, Jerry, during her frenzy since our father had passed away some months before. Wouldn't it make sense to call the patriarch?

I decided that Jerry should not miss out on this problem-solving journey and that he certainly would want to get at least partial credit for resolving this urgent family crisis. While he actually wanted to do none of those things, he did agree to travel with me to my sister's distant land and see what the hell was going on. As it turned out, sweet sis had also called him with a very similar opening statement previously noted. So off we went.

As we drove, we discussed how Dede could become overwrought with emotion. We decided that her description of her ex-husband's being there, along with her harebrained idea that Mema had cut the tires on her car, was probably the result of temporary insanity. We knew we would sort through this and find that, while some type of unpleasant event had actually transpired, the real details would be substantially different from those described over the phone.

After our father died in 1977, Mema had taken it upon herself to be the overseer of all of our sister's activities. When Kenny and sis parted ways the first time, Mema decided that he must be advised of his unacceptable behavior, and she was the only logical person to handle the matter. Mema drove around town looking for this guy who had abandoned her daughter, and she eventually discovered where the rascal was holed up. She knocked on the door and asked to see him and requested he come out to her car.

Once at the car, Mema said, "Listen, dumb ass, if my husband was still alive, he would have tracked you down and beat the crap out of you for the way you have treated our daughter. But he's not here, and so I had to tell you how we feel, and you should never come around our daughter again!" It was from that day forward that the ex was fondly referred to as D. A. Kenny, in honor of Mema's lecture and her lasting opinion of her off-again, on-again son-in-law.

Mema had established herself as the parent-in-charge, and we did not expect to find the chaos that had been verbally described by our dear sister when Jerry and I arrived at the apartment. But as we pulled onto her street, there at the curb was the red Volkswagen Beetle with all four tires flat as a pancake. Our conviction that we could improve this situation began to lose steam, just as the air had found its way out of the VW's tires.

I suggested that we just go in and hear from our little sister. And sure enough, there was D. A. Kenny sitting right there in the apartment, looking like a wet puppy that had been brought in from a rainstorm. Uh, make that a hailstorm. Dede looked like she could have been crying for about two weeks rather than one day.

I can still hear the stereo's pleasant guitar music playing quietly in the background as we were told that all was well between the two lovers, and they had made a mistake when they divorced. Now the planets were aligned, and they wanted to be together again. Somewhere during their side of the story, Jerry started humming along with the guitar music, and I began thinking how I really wanted to go back outside one more time to make sure my eyes had not deceived me regarding four flat tires. The story continued to the point where Mema had come to the apartment, asked if they were getting back together, heard the answer, clearly expressed her opinion, and left. She then went to her car, got something out of the glove box, walked around the VW, briefly stopping at each tire, then climbed into her car, and left. The VW sank onto the pavement, and Dede called us with a jumbled version of what had just transpired.

When they finished the update of the pending reunion and the Mema incident, Jerry and I took care of our required brotherly role-playing duties. First, I told D. A. Kenny that he better treat our sister right this time or we *all* would come looking for him. (He didn't and we didn't.) The patriarch then wanted to know if D. A. had a job, if could he support Dede, and if he had stopped his childish ways. He then finished with other "social workisms" necessary to gather data for a later report. We gave the couple a hug and wished them luck because we knew they were really going to need it.

At last, we were allowed to go back outside and inspect the crime scene. It didn't really take too long to look at a flat tire, but maybe a little longer than usual, because all four tires were in a similar condition. Jerry and I quickly overcame the urge to raise the hood and check out the engine and decided that it was now time to go to Mema's house for the rest of the story.

Mema worked in the appliance sales department at the big Sears store at the mall, but she was home when we arrived. Although she was not expecting to see us, she was not surprised by our visit nor did it take long for her to begin talking about what had happened.

During her story, we finally were able to establish the relationship between Dede and her ex to the flat tires on the VW. Mema told us she had recently purchased four new Sears tires for the VW to help with the finances of our once-again-single sister. During the morning break at Sears, a coworker innocently asked Mema, "Did I see Kenny driving Dede's red VW today [she was not privileged to the D. A. Kenny part]? Have they gotten back together?"

This information was all Mema needed to seriously peak her interest in finding out just what was going on over there in that apartment. She dutifully remained at her post in the appliance department until her appointed lunch break but wasted no time getting to the apartment to investigate. She went into the apartment and, of course, was greeted by the happy couple who reluctantly shared their story.

Mema ignored the music and quickly discovered they intended to get back together. She did not like it and made sure they knew how she felt in no uncertain terms. She added, "There was no way in this world that D. A.

Kenny is going to ride around in the red VW on the four new Sears tires that I have bought with my hard-earned money!" (I don't think we have seen Mema cry but about four times, but when she was telling us this part, the tears did flow, even if for only for a moment.)

Mema then left the apartment, went out to her car, got an ice pick from the car's glove box, and proceeded to jab a hole into each and every tire, making a hole that was big enough to ensure that all the air would escape. She got back into her car and returned to work.

Jerry and I experienced an immediate "Aha!" moment. For as crazy as this story seemed, it now made sense, or at least it provided a rational reason for an irrational behavior. The *Love Bug* had been grounded.

Mema was upset, but our assessment was that she was not going to have to be committed. Dede was upset but was trying to get her life back together. Jerry and I were upset because we had thought for a minute that we could solve this problem. We decided we needed to get out of town immediately, for this was no place for the boys to be in the middle of a mother-daughter conflict. No one was ever going to believe the story, and even if we tried to tell it, people would think Mema had gone off the deep end. If we got back soon enough, maybe no one would miss us, and we wouldn't have to tell where we had been. However, we were asked a lot of questions when we returned, and we agreed that this was a Mema moment to be shared.

Oh, I almost forgot. I need to answer the most often asked question about this story. "Why in the world does someone carry an ice pick in the glove box?" Well, Mema loved to fish. She and her friend Joyce went fishing almost every week. That meant that every week, Mema stopped at the store to buy bait and broke up ice for the cooler. So what? Don't you have an ice pick in your glove box?

EVERY TIME I FEEL THE SPIRIT

Most families living in the Deep South during the 1950s regularly went to church. Growing up near the community of Raymond, Georgia, was no exception; and our mother believed that her four sons, and later one daughter, needed to attend church. Mother was raised a Baptist, which provided all the guidance she would need to determine which denomination was appropriate for her family.

Our father supported getting the kids up and ready for Sunday school, but he never actually went along. His mother—Nanny White to us—was a formidable, devout believer who never missed a single opportunity to be at her Pentecostal Holiness Church. I think they worshipped the same Jesus that we did over in the Baptist Church, but when we visited our grandmother's church, we were always more than a little nervous about the way they expressed their belief. Their church prayed kneeling at the pew, kneeling at the front altar, standing and saying words we could not understand while waving their hands in the air, and all the while a big man seated in an oversized chair located on the right side of the pulpit frequently acknowledged all these behaviors with a deep-voiced "Amen" or "Yes, Lord." The preacher spoke much louder than our Baptist minister, who could get pretty loud on his own, but Nanny White's minister never left any doubt where you would end up if you had even a little sin in your life.

I'm confident that my father chose not to go to church because he had heard about as much as required for an entire lifetime during his early years growing up under the stern tutorage of his mother. Since our mother wanted us to go, she had to take us and make sure that we went into the Sunday school rooms and sat in the congregation in easy reach should we begin to wiggle too much during the sermons.

The Raymond Baptist Church was very typical of churches during that era. The structure was a white wooden-framed building centered by a double door front entrance, along with windows evenly spaced on either side. There was a large steeple on the roof with a cross on the top, which also housed the church bell that was rung by hand via a rope running from the bell through the ceiling into the vestibule. There were several small classrooms located behind the chapel and a long permanent picnic table behind the church for frequent dinner-on-the-ground events.

Since the minister was paid a meager salary, members of the congregation were encouraged to extend an invitation to Sunday dinner to help cover his expenses. Only once do I remember having the preacher over for Sunday lunch. It was a significant time for us because it was such a rare occurrence. But we were on our best behavior and, after the meal, invited the preacher outside to throw horseshoes. On Sunday evening, he even mentioned our family and the horseshoes during his sermon. It wasn't the kind of thing that made Daddy start back to church, but Mother was content knowing we had done the right thing.

One Sunday morning, I was seated in church on the end of the second pew from the front. I was ten years old and had been to enough church services to know the routine. We would hear a few reports about how many were in Sunday school and how much money had been given. We then sang a few songs, passed around the offering plate, and the preacher would share a sermon. About three major points tying the scripture to some real-life example, along with an occasional poem, would usually cover the spiritual needs of the congregation; and we could leave and were set for another week. But before you left, there was an opportunity to walk down to the front during an invitational hymn if you wanted to have a short prayer with the preacher or if you wanted to be saved. The Baptist were big on being saved, and the church members were given adequate time to make up their mind while several verses of the last hymn were being sung. Sometimes, the preacher would stop a song and say that he felt someone in the congregation was struggling with a decision and asked that we sing several more verses just to give that person chance to resolve their dilemma. We would look around to see if we could tell who that struggling person might be. Maybe we expected to see some sort of scrunched up face on a person in emotional pain or notice if someone was crying, but usually, everybody looked about the same, and no one came down during those extra verses. But on this particular Sunday, I had this unusual thought during the very first verse that I ought to move right out into the aisle and go over and shake the preacher's hand and accept Jesus. I don't recall anyone telling me that I really needed to do this. Mother had not advised me nor did the preacher hit on some dreaded sin that grabbed the attention of a ten-year-old that would send me to the front to escape the gates of hell. I just thought it was the right thing to do. I wondered how things would feel differently after I got home or after I went back to school, but most everything seemed to stay about the same.

A few days later, a lady from the church called to say that I was to be baptized on a Sunday night two weeks later. I was directed to wear a white shirt, to bring a towel and a change of clothes, and to please arrive early so the preacher could meet with those being immersed to explain what we were supposed to do. There were about four of us to be baptized that Sunday night. The preacher told us to walk down into the baptismal pool, and he would say a few things about each of us. He then would place his right hand behind our neck and cover our nose with a cloth with his left hand. We were to hold on to his left arm and let him lean us back and immerse us in the water. Seemed like a simple plan. There was a large man who went right before me. I was impressed that the preacher could hold him under and raise him back up without both of them having to thrash a little bit to keep their footing. I also noticed that the big man had a cloth that the preacher used to cover the man's nose and mouth. I only had my towel.

I don't remember much about what the preacher said. I could only see that he was holding my towel in his left hand that could mean just one thing: my towel was going to be baptized that very night right along with me. Sure enough, down I went, up I came and climbed out of the pool with my new life and a soaked towel. I mostly drip-dried that evening but eventually was able to get into dry clothes and come back into the sanctuary for the preacher's sermon. He wore waders under his robe and quickly changed back to his coat and tie. I never got to ask him why in the world he had used my only drying towel for my immersion. Maybe he wanted me to always remember the night I was baptized. I suppose it worked very well.

We continued to attend a Baptist church for years to come. After we moved to Columbus, we were members of the Hilton Terrace Baptist Church, which I attended until the time I left home to attend college. I made many friends at the church and, as a teenager, was involved in all the activities.

I was in the Royal Ambassadors, sang in the choir, and attended most of the church-sponsored social events. At fifteen, I became more interested in church than I thought possible after the night when Sandra McRae hit me on the back of the head as she walked behind my pew and gave me the cutest little smile a young boy could ever hope for.

The church provided a social outlet for me and provided a great excuse for me not to be at home and having to deal with the very unsociable behavior of my father, especially on weekends. As unchurched as he was, he did come to my rescue when Mother decided we needed to attend a church closer to our house. We visited a nearby church twice. I was in teenage misery with thoughts of moving away from my church friends. I was pleading my case once again to my mother after the second visit to what was destined to become our new church. My father stood up and looked at my mother and me and firmly stated, "We need to stay at the church where we are members." I had only seen my father once at our church, but surprisingly enough, his word was final, and we never entertained moving to another church again. I sang "Hallelujah" and "Praise the Lord" all day long because of the uplifting spirit I experienced. I did not sing those cheerful songs around Mother, for I did remember my place in the pecking order.

After I became old enough to drive, it was never an issue again. I would note that it was never an issue for Mother again. She remained a staunch member at Hilton Terrace for the remainder of her life, and the pastor there at the time of her death conducted her funeral services, and her Sunday school class served as honorary pallbearers.

I may not want my children and grandchildren knowing about all the church-related activities I was involved in. There were many opportunities for fun and a little mischief as we grew up together with close friends and family. Joe, Steve, Allen, Sandra, and others helped establish relationships that provided a foundation for trying to be a good boy and to enjoy life.

The influence of the church family continued into college. I attended two Baptist-supported colleges: a two-year junior college, Truett-McConnell, and later received a BA degree from Shorter College. During those postsecondary years, I discovered that I truly enjoyed music and actually earned an associate degree in that field of study. I'm not so sure whether music was my original plan, but it became increasingly important as I signed up for classes that very first college quarter. By the time the Ws got to the registration table, there was no space in the other classes I had hoped to get into. So I took some music classes and simply kept going from there.

Singing in the college choir was a good experience, and I also took voice and piano lessons. Keep in mind that when I started this in college, I had never read a note of music before in my life. Some of the professors really enjoyed hearing a nineteen-year-old play from Schumann's beginner's piano book. My voice teacher also wanted to know if I had ever had problems with my hearing. It was a great start, but it didn't dawn on me until several years later that actual musical talent was an important criterion for majoring in music.

Ted Holley was an older student who worked for several years in business and decided on going to college to study for the ministry. He asked me one day during the winter of 1966 if I would go with him up to his little church near Hiawassee to lead the singing. We determined that I had to start somewhere, and a tiny church hidden in the mountains seemed like a good place. I drove Ted's car that Sunday morning while Ted reviewed his sermon notes. I enjoyed driving along the winding roads on the mountains between the campus and Hiawassee. Finally, Ted asked me to slow down because he said he had read the same scripture verse four times while trying to decide which of the mountain curves was to be his last. We arrived, and I led the singing and sang "Amazing Grace" as a solo from the hymnal. It was terrible, but the kind members of the church appreciated having young people come up and be part of their small congregation. The big payoff for my first music-directing experience was having the opportunity to eat Sunday lunch with a couple from the church. Ted ate with some member of the congregation almost every Sunday, but for me, it was a great break from the school cafeteria. The visit was also highlighted by the mountain scene from their home. The barn, horses, pasture in the valley, and mountains in the background were truly picture-perfect.

There were many opportunities to lead the singing in churches all over the area. Once, I heard the term *tune hyster* used because the leader raised up songs for the congregation. I can't find the term written anywhere, but I knew when it was used, it was directed at me. Once I had a small choir sing a hymn while the offering plates were passed around. During the "special music," the ushers just came right on up into the choir loft to pass the offering plate through the choir as we sang. Several of the men tried to get to their wallets to retrieve some cash while holding on to their hymnal and continue singing. I kept waving my arms while trying to imagine what kind of Sunday lunch might be required to make up for this experience. Another time, I was working for a small church located about fifteen miles from the college campus and agreed to lead the singing and direct the choir for a weeklong revival. Since there was a guest evangelist, I thought that meant I was to be guest choir director. Following the final service of the revival, the pastor called me aside and took out his personal wallet and handed me a five-dollar bill. He said that all the money collected during the week had to go to the visiting preacher, but he really appreciated me coming over and leading the singing.

Later that spring, I was called into the president's office to meet with a pastor and deacon from a church in Calhoun, Georgia. A request to go the president's office was not unusual and meant that some type of good public relation work was under way. This was not to be confused with being called into the dean's office, which was usually highlighted by a question regarding an unacceptable behavior being investigated. I had visited both offices before. But in this instance, I was interviewed and requested to come to Calhoun one weekend for a trial visit in consideration of directing a youth choir and coordinating a summer youth program. Following the instructions given to me, I hitched a ride and was delivered to the front of a local drugstore. I went in and placed my suitcase in aisle 3 and stood for about twenty minutes, wondering what was to come next. Sure enough, the deacon I had met earlier was also the local druggist and came over to welcome me. He later introduced me to several other church members and took me over to the pastor's house where I stayed for the weekend. The visit went very well, and I was invited to come live in Calhoun for the summer and worked in the Belmont Baptist Church.

During the summer, I lived in a single room of a boarding house with a shared bathroom down the hall. An elderly widow rented three rooms of her large house, which was located next to a funeral home. The landlady was delightful and provided breakfast for me each day, which was the only meal that came with the room. When I would come into the kitchen, she would put her teeth in and talk with me. A couple of times I caught her without her teeth nearby, and I would need to wait until she retrieved them before we began our little talk. Sometimes, I helped with the feeding of a monkey she kept in an outside cage in the backyard or with walking her blind poodle. Both animals she got from one of her adult children who wanted to know if she could keep them for a while until they could get a bigger place. The daughter must have been unable to find anything bigger because they were still there when I returned to college at the end of August.

I did get another real-paying job as choir director at the Hills Crossing Baptist Church during my sophomore year in college. I received a check for twenty-five dollars each week for one Wednesday night rehearsal and two services on Sunday, as well as helping out with the youth program. The first month of the year that had a fifth Sunday in the month, I discovered that the agreement was specifically one hundred dollars per month, and any fifth Sunday work was gratis. But for me, a hundred dollars a month made the car payment, put gas in the car, and allowed an occasional visit to the Tastee-Freez next to the college campus. I continued to learn and appreciate church music methods and, as you might understand, I came to realize that for the most part, there is not much money to be earned in the vocation of serving the Lord.

As I was making plans to move to the Atlanta area in order to attend another college, the pastor and local druggist deacon from Calhoun returned to offer a deal I couldn't refuse: a full-time choir and youth director's job and time for me to continue my studies at the nearby Shorter College in Rome. One of the ministerial students told me that such an unexpected offer had to be the spirit of the Lord, and I should follow the path laid out for me. While I was unsure about this, I did choose to go with the flow and take advantage of a sure thing, which included a paying job while I went to school. I auditioned and was accepted into Shorter College's music program with a major in voice and church music. I sang Handel's "Si tra i ceppi" for the audition. The reviewing faculty did not know it was the only foreign language piece I had ever worked on, and I had little clue as to the meaning of the words. But the audition result once again provided for the directing of a church choir, and I could continue singing in the Shorter College Chorale. As my music skills and the requirements for a successful music major grew apart, my expert training as the choir's bus driver assured me of staying an active member of the Chorale, even though my music major days were limited.

By the second semester at Shorter, I had changed from music to psychology and sociology. Any chance for divine intervention was thwarted by Mr. J's music theory and sight-singing class. I was headed in another direction. I finished the sociology degree but ended up teaching in 1970. We moved to the Atlanta area in the summer of 1971. I worked for the Woodland Hills Baptist Church for a few months and eventually settled in for about nine years coordinating a youth and music program at the Ash Street Baptist Church.

We were able to build the Ash Street Youth Program from about twenty hardy souls to almost one hundred high school and college students who attended. The church sponsored five major youth mission trips to Arizon. (three), Connecticut, and Texas. Singing, teaching, evangelism, and soul-searching were a significant part of my leadership responsibilities. There may be another entire chapter or possibly a book worth of experiences that connect those young people to some inner spirit. Some of the kids later went into the full-time ministry or music ministry, growing out of their connection to the church and especially the mission trips. My own inner spirit was leading toward less time at church and more time in my job and a desire to seek a doctoral degree in education.

In those years, I was trying to discern the relationship between what I was doing in the Baptist Church with the bigger spiritual picture of goodness throughout the world. A friend at work brought me a copy of the 1961 classic by Robert Heinlein, *Stranger in a Strange Land.* It provided the groundwork for questions to be asked about religious groups and at least provided me an opportunity to broaden the definition of works of the spirit in all religions. Oddly enough, Stephen King's *The Stand* provided a clearer understanding of good versus evil than I could have ever imagined on my own. A clearer definition of the spirit was provided by real people in the real world. I discovered the Baptist did not take kindly to an action of divorce. The divorce was not only from my former wife, but also seemed to include almost all the good Baptists in the church as well. While the breakup between the two of us may not be different from many similar separations, the impact on the *spirit* of kindness, love, and forgiveness took a beating.

I rebounded nicely through membership in a couple of Presbyterian churches. I quickly discovered that the spirit was located where one looked and was not permanently lost based on any personal screwups an individual may have had to slog through. Two years later, Lynda and I were married in a Presbyterian church, and the inner-self "rocky road" began to smooth out for both of us. We both served on committees, and I sang in choirs during our many years working in Marietta. Later, we moved to Jackson, Georgia, in 1997; we became members of the local Methodist church, where I directed the choir for about five years.

Having only lived in the South, it certainly seems that organized Protestant churches play a significant role in the lives of families throughout the Bible Belt. In time of need, we cannot discount the importance of an uplifting spirit provided by pastors and members of the congregation. The good Protestants, however, do not control the spiritual market because of

similar worldwide examples of goodness. Nor (here goes,
it) can the entire population be served by a single human
...ple for the guide to life here and in the hereafter. I finally had to
resolve the complexities of the path of the spirit in as simplistic terms as
I could discern. It has become, for me, the *mountain theory*.

A mountaintop easily represents the spiritual peak sought by many
who believe that goodness, kindness, care for our fellowman, self-control,
patience, and avoidance of evil should be practical matters in one's
life. Developing these traits and skills is a work in progress that may
be characterized as a path to be taken or, more accurately, a path to be
chosen. We may walk, run, or climb these pathways as we grow and come to
understand such things of the spirit. The pathways ultimately lead upward
toward a summit available to all. The paths may be parallel to others of
similar faiths. The paths may cross over or wind about in uncertain ways.
There are other paths leading up that we never see nor have ever heard
about, yet they lead upward just the same. Finally, when we arrive at the
top, we most assuredly are going to be made aware of others who are there.
Some we may know. Many, many others will arrive from differing faiths,
beliefs, gods, symbols, and rituals that we have never known.

You might imagine that the mountain theory goes over big in my
southern church. For most part, I have kept this idea to myself and only
once, while teaching adult Sunday school, did I catch myself drawing stick
figures walking up a hill before the class realized where I was headed. I
acknowledged that the topic would be for another day, and I quickly moved
back to the original lesson. The point doesn't need to be argued as to how
you go about the journey, but only consider that each of us should try to
take such a trip in our lives.

We should realize the value of religion for all individuals and families
for it provides the duct tape for holding society together. Whatever may
be the deeper truth of the spirit, I may never know. I only know that at the
age of ten, I experienced a feeling of rightness in a journey of about twenty
feet as I began a walk on my own spiritual pathway.

I'M FROM THE STATE
AND I'M HERE TO HELP YOU

I stood in the elevator with a large brown suitcase thinking to myself, "What the heck have I gotten myself into?" It was my first day working for the Georgia Department of Education in the fall of 1976. I distinctly recall during my job interview that there would be very little travel, and most of it would include day trips to school systems within driving distance. But I had received a call the day before I was to report for work and told that I needed to go overnight to Valdosta with my boss and the program director.

This day was a day of firsts for me beginning with my first day on a new job in downtown Atlanta. Downtown meant driving north from Clayton County into Atlanta and sharing the road with hundreds of cars that were all trying to beat me to a parking place.

Second, I was expected to pack for an overnight business trip. All I had was a rather ugly, laminate-looking brown suitcase. I never had needed a simple carry-on suit bag. Of course my boss and the director had done this many times, and each had their classy black bag to throw over the shoulder, allowing them to maintain tight meeting and flight schedules. The overall presentation of the brown suitcase was enhanced with a Truett-McConnell Junior College bumper sticker, which helped date the suitcase over ten years when the large suitcase held all my clothing for the journey back and forth between home and school.

So how could I add awkwardness to this opening day? That was easy; we were scheduled to *fly* to Valdosta, Georgia. I had never flown, and now I was to delay my new bosses by having them stand around while I checked and went through baggage claim with ol' Big Brown. The only good news, if you can call it that, was the airport at the time was the old Atlanta Hartsfield, and security meant that no one carried onto the plane a visible handgun in their waistband. We were scheduled to fly Southern Airways on a two-engine prop that was boarded and exited via a small fold-down stairway lowered from the rear of the aircraft. We flew from Atlanta, to Columbus, to Albany, to Moultrie, and, finally, to Valdosta. The I-75 route was not complete at the time, and flying was supposed to be the fastest way.

I gradually recovered from the country-come-to-town look on my first day and began to settle into my new job. One of my first responsibilities was to coordinate a federal grant program implemented in conjunction with the colleges and universities. The State Department of Education regularly hosted meetings of all the university department heads to discuss the funding cycle, estimates of money for the following year, and several other equally exciting topics. I had to prepare the agenda, schedule the meeting room, and facilitate the discussion.

Although I had long since buried the ugly brown suitcase in my backyard, I remained intimidated by all the PhDs that encircled the room at these meetings. Every university representative was "Doctor" somebody. While my master's degree allowed me to occupy the same room, it could not lift me to the lofty self-assessment of the professors. These meetings turned out to be very significant for me, however, as we worked through grants and several meetings, it became quite clear that these fine educators seemed to have one skill that was noteworthy. Each of them somehow persevered by completing a dissertation at a major university. I distinctly remember near the end of a meeting actually whispering to myself, "You know, if these guys have gotten a doctorate, there is no reason in the world that I can't get one!" It was that day I began down a path where I was sure I could attain much-higher goals in education. Within months, I completed the application and assessments required to enter the University of Georgia's education doctoral program. Seven short years later, I graduated from the UGA with a doctorate in education leadership.

Most of those years I worked at the Department of Education, we were led by State Superintendent Dr. Charles McDaniel. Having come through the ranks of a variety of teaching and administrative positions, Dr. Mac was a classic educational leader. Additionally he was a gentleman of solid family commitments and stringent Southern values. I was coordinating one of our annual conferences in Gainesville one fall, and we were pleased to have Dr. Mac accept our invitation from the numerous requests he received, and he agreed to keynote our general session. The state superintendent of schools was an impressive draw for our statewide group of special education administrators.

We had planned and worked hard to have everything in place necessary for a smooth operation at the Holiday Inn conference center. Everything proceeded as planned through the introductions and first speaker of the session. Just as Dr. McDaniel came to the podium, I noticed that we could overhear a quiet murmur of conversations in the adjoining conference room. This was not unexpected because the rooms were divided by those giant accordion-style fold-out walls that hang from the ceiling but don't quite reach the floor necessary to diminish the sound coming from your neighbor. But as Dr. Mac was making the second point of his speech, the piano in the room next door began to play, and soon there were many women's voices singing "Shall We Gather at the River." It was loud enough that Dr. Mac had to increase his volume to be heard. Several people in the audience were either looking over their shoulders as if they might see something through the curtain or they sat tapping their toes to the beat of the music.

As conference coordinator, I was immediately dispatched to see if we might get some relief from the vocal intrusion. Once in the hallway, I saw the large sign indicating the "Women Aglow Luncheon." Our competition was a local chapter of the national organization for Christian women. I hoped that the gathering at the river would immediately lead to the salad bar and their meal. I opened the door and stepped inside just as the leader said, "For our next two songs, look on the back of your song sheet." As I left the Aglow room, I was trying to decide if somehow I might be able to gather my things and sneak out to the parking lot and disappear. Instead I returned and asked that we increase the volume of the microphone and take the songfest head-on. Dr. Mac and the final song ended about the same time. His closing remarks were positive, and he provided a short humorous story about teaching in a variety of environments. He left quickly and without further comment.

Several months later, I did have an unexpected opportunity to drive Dr. McDaniel to a retirement reception about eighty miles southeast of Atlanta. His regular assistant had a conflict, and I was nominated and elected without any formal vote. He did share a chuckle with me about his speech that day, and we had a pleasant afternoon at the reception for a forty-year teaching veteran. As we returned to the car, Dr. Mac said, "Alan, you may feel free to return to Atlanta without unnecessary delay." I thought about that comment for a while. It was typical Dr. Mac in his controlled manner. I had never before been told to "haul ass" in such a distinguished manner.

Our department within the education bureaucracy handled federal programs for disabled students. In the late 1970s and '80s, there were many changes and regulations impacting the local school system. As a result, we often were at the center of attention for interpreting the laws and regulations surrounding special education. Many of the employees were quite serious about their role, and few relied on humor to ease the stress placed on them by superiors, deadlines, and self-imposed neuroses. That was not the case with me and a few select individuals who worked hard at being successful in our responsibilities but routinely found or created laughter when we could.

Sometimes a simple question could create a bureaucratic uproar up and down the chain of command. The chain was well-defined. For example, only coordinators and directors could have office doors. Employees who were moved into those positions changed offices. I watched maintenance remove a door from a lowly consultant's office and move it eighteen feet across the suite to the office to be occupied by a new coordinator. So when I arrived to this new place in my leisure suit and tie, I soon realized that we had to offer comic relief to help keep things in perspective.

But let's get back to the questions. We were all puzzled when one of the consultants reported that one of the local school administrators had called him and wanted to know what to do with forty cases of headlights. He responded, "Why are you calling me about headlights? Did you spend federal money to purchase them?" There was a pause, and "Mike, you're in charge of hospital homebound services. We have forty cases of *head lice*: lice, not lights. What do we do?" We whooped as he told the story. It was even funnier when he admitted that he was unsure about how to resolve her problem even after he understood. During many meetings after that, several would obviously scratch their heads during discussions to keep the story alive.

Falling under the heading of "You Can't Make This Stuff Up," I shared a recent conversation with a local superintendent following a meeting in Dalton, Georgia. The South Georgia school superintendent was appointed to the committee by the State Board of Education, which I believed to add at least some level of respectability to the position. The committee members had a tendency to rely on state staff to take care of their every need. Still I was taken aback when Billy called to say, "Alan, can you call the Holiday Inn and see if I left my gun in the room?" I responded, "Say that again, Billy." Of course he said it exactly the same way and then added, "I must have left it under the mattress. You know, you can never be sure about the kind of place you'll be staying when you are away from home." He must have found his pistol in some dirty clothes because he never called me back.

Finally I shared a call received from the state superintendent of schools. I must remind the readers that state bureaucracy called for information to travel via specific channels; never did the main man call down to a four-time-removed coordinator. I answered the phone and a familiar voice said, "Alan, this is Charlie Mac. Listen, do we have beds in schools?" My very first thought was this really is my good friend Larry in a nearby office trying to pull a little prank. I almost provided a rather smart-ass answer about the principal and the secretary needing a bed from time to time, but thank goodness, I stopped just short of disaster. Instead I said, "Well, Dr. Mac, I don't believe we do have beds in schools." As it turned out, the question really had to do with approval of federal money for the disabled. Some school-age children who were being moved into the public school for the first time did in fact need cots or small beds due to physical disabilities.

The experiences at the Department of Education were wonderful opportunities to interact with good school administrators in school systems and colleges around the state. Professionally, I grew confident in managing federal and state regulations as well as the many budget issues associated with the programs for the disabled. The job requirements allowed me to move up through the ranks and even have my own door until we moved into the new Twin Towers where everyone was assigned a cubicle. We were directed not to tape, glue, and pin or nail anything to the six-foot-high cage walls. I did have one small sign hanging near my desk: "In every bureaucracy there always one person who knows everything. This person must be fired." The cubicle wall seemed to be the best place for the sign.

State employees are notorious for meetings, conferences, retreats, forums, and a host of other words that generally mean to sit around and expound. We were experts at writing plans with important goals and objectives. Many times the writing sessions included overnight trips that often lead to serious relaxation efforts when we finished for the day. If there were late-night pranks or other mischief, Larry and I often received credit for tomfoolery regardless of our involvement. There were simple acts such as entering the room of a new staff person to remove all the lightbulbs to create a visual challenge when they returned from the after-dinner social gathering.

We once were working all day in a cabin away from the main lodge. We had papers with copious notes scattered around the sitting area. Bob, a coordinator with his own office door, arrived late in the afternoon and was to occupy the cabin for the next two days. He walked in with a young lady from another state agency and rudely suggested that we go ahead and move back over to the lodge. We determined that there must have been a prearrangement for close-quartered interagency planning, and the sooner we gathered our supplies and left, the better for such cooperative activity. We were not in the least disturbed by the actions of consenting adults, but were more than mildly perturbed by the disrespect we received from our coworker.

At the main lodge breakfast table the next morning, Bob was extremely unhappy. He was fuming over the fact that some unknown persons had completely covered his lady friend's Cadillac with toilet paper. Larry and I absolutely ignored any implication or knowledge of the event, leaving our friend to direct his unkind remarks to Janet who was another candidate for having pulled a prank. She didn't deny the accusation because her thinking was quite muddled as a result of several encounters with a wineglass the night before. Consequently, I was no longer the prime suspect, and Janet didn't actually remember why Bob did not speak to her for several weeks.

As much as I would like to take credit for well-thought-out practical jokes, there was an instant where I can only give credit to a coworker. The story evolves following the appointment of a new director of our department. He followed a longtime fixture in the state agency that left a huge gap in the understanding of the history of the special needs program in Georgia. The new director was perceived to be more than casually self-confident and fell into the role of "I am your leader, we'll go this way," quite easily. One of my coworkers obtained an eight-by-ten black-and-white glossy photo of the current governor of Georgia. She wrote, "Art, welcome to the Department," and signed it "George Busby." The picture was placed in a frame and sent via interoffice mail to the new boss. We were sure he would find humor in a little welcoming gag. We could have taken all the lights out of his office, for goodness' sake. But he didn't catch the receipt of the gift as a stunt and placed the signed photo for all to see on a bookshelf in his office. As long as I worked in that building, the governor's photo stood on the top shelf. No one said a word, but it never helped us focus on more serious matters when meeting in his office and having George stare down at us. I think someone finally mentioned to him that it could be a well-intended joke, for after we moved into the new building, I never saw the governor's face again in his office.

I eventually left the Department of Education in 1983 to work in a local school system. It turned out to be a great decision for me because I discovered I could never change the course of the bureaucracy but could make a difference in a local school district. I will, however, always be grateful for the opportunity to learn so much and see many places in the state as a state employee. Of course I would have never seen and heard Larry's classic story of the "Big Daddy Rabbit" as only Larry could demonstrate. I believe that this story remains the property of Larry, and it is a very good place to end this chapter.

OH, YOU BETTER WATCH OUT

The celebration of Christmas has always been a special time in our family. I never heard my mother tell us why she was so intent on making sure all of us had special gifts at Christmas, but she made a big deal of the occasion, even if there were only a few inexpensive presents. I remember getting at least one gift from my wish list, which was clearly marked by a folded corner of the page and circled in the big Sears, Roebuck and Co. catalog. I also recall getting one unexpected gift almost every year, making me wonder how Santa knew to bring me a watch, for example, when it hadn't been on the list. The last gift to be opened was the stocking that was hung on the mantle. Each of us had our own long sock loaded with an apple, orange, a box of raisins, walnuts, pecans, pieces of candy, and other special treats that we normally did not have during the year. Christmas mornings also provided those ghastly black-and-white photos of us in our pajamas along with opened boxes and paper scattered on the floor; our hair sticking out in odd places; wearing a cowboy hat, new sweater, or real Indian moccasins; looking at the directions for a model plane, erector set, "My First Chemistry Lab," or dozens of pieces from "Fort Apache."

Mother regularly took photos with her little camera, but when our uncle Doug showed up at Christmas, he always had to demonstrate the latest photo technology. His early cameras were the roll-type film in a fancy-schmancy Ansco, foldout model with a lot of dials and shutter speeds. Doug was an early Polaroid enthusiast, and we were amazed at watching our present-opening photo develop right before our eyes in mere sixty seconds. Every year was marked by a new Polaroid that was faster and with much-improved color. For a couple of years, he lugged cables, cords, and a twin floodlight bar to take moving pictures right in our own home. Months later, when we visited our uncle and got to see those movies, we thought we looked goofy and were generally embarrassed that we danced, made faces, and Hula-hooped on live film. In the end, it seemed that photo slides were our uncle's forte because after many years of poses, there were boxes of slides found in his garage. We only hope that the 8 mm Hula-hoop films have long since expired.

As adults, Christmas meant going to Mother's for lunch, followed by the opening of presents, and of course, stockings were hung on the door for every child. After the first grandchild, the family event was staged for several years at Jerry and Cindy's house. There was a period of time in the mid- to late-1970s when the routine also included going to the airport to pick up my brothers Jim and Thom, who lived in Pennsylvania at the time. From there, I was to take them to the host sibling's for the great bedlam associated with present opening. I was assigned this duty for several years in a row and found satisfaction in instigating some unexpected surprises when the brothers deplaned.

During the airport connection years, I was serving as a youth director in a local church. In the group, I realized we had quite a few young people who were current or past members of the high school band. While discussing the flight and arrival times with one of my brothers, I said, "Well, we look forward to having you here. I will be sure to have the band and media there for your arrival." Thus began the plan. As it turned out, we had eleven band instruments and two "reporters" with notepad and a camera. Large signs were made welcoming Jim and Thom home. Many travelers stopped by to ask who these important people were coming into Atlanta/Hartsfield International. We replied, "Jim and Thom, you know the singers?" "Oh yes," they responded as if they recalled knowing about the stars. As the boys came off the plane, the band began to play John Philip Sousa's "Washington Post." Our reporters rushed to the guys and began asking them about the flight, taking photos, etc. It was quite a reception. Of course, in today's airports, you couldn't get that many musical instruments past security in time to meet the flight.

My brothers chuckled and enjoyed the attention, but then threatened to get even if I ever did anything like that again. The very next year, I got clear instructions: "Come alone if you know what's good for you." I did.

Only that year, I dressed as Santa Claus with red coat, beard, boots, and hat. It was the whole deal. This great idea had two major flaws. First, our children were very young and still believed. Seeing Dad dressed as Santa was confusing, and they could not quite figure out how I could look so much like the real thing, but still be Dad in costume. This took a lot of explanation and assurance that I was not going to negatively influence the real jolly old St. Nick from showing up on Christmas Eve.

The second flaw in the plan came when I arrived at the airport. It never dawned on me that every child in the place would want to come over and see Santa. I had no candy or bag of presents. I was a nice Santa and did listen to the wishes of two or three children. When I arrived at the gate, I discovered the plane was one and one-half hours late, resulting in Santa standing in the terminal waving and talking to children and adults. Many travelers assumed I was the official Delta Santa, and several stopped to request information on flight arrival, delays, and gate information. Finally, the boys showed up and walked right past me without giving Santa a second look. So I said nothing and just followed them through the terminal to the baggage claim area. All the time, they were looking around, wary of the band, but searching for their ride. I finally walked closer and asked if I could give them a ride home in my sleigh. I may have looked like Santa, but my voice and Southern accent are unmistakable. It was a fun ride home and kicked off a great Christmas season for our family.

There really isn't much to compare to the combination of joy and frustration of being Santa for your children. Many challenges are presented to Santa parents, like what to buy, how to secure the money for the holidays, wrapping all the presents, baking, balancing a jam-packed schedule between Thanksgiving and Christmas, what to give Uncle Thom, where to hide the goodies, and finally, putting things together after we have finally got the kids in bed. The assembly list goes on and on. Jerry had sixty-four coiled springs required for assembling the trampoline for his son. The work took place outside until 1:00 a.m. in a rain that began to turn to snow.

I couldn't quite find all the pieces for Alexis's swing set. As we were swinging in the backyard on Christmas morning, that swing set initiated the great Santa question. We could see the question coming in her eyes. She looked at the two swings, the sliding board, and the teeter-totter (a two-seat swing). All the while, she was wondering how the sleigh, chimney, and bag of toys actually could have resulted in getting a playground erected in her backyard. She finally asked, "Are your parents Santa Claus?" For our children and grandchildren, the answer has always been the same: "As long as you believe, there will always be a Santa Claus."

Having only girls in the house at Christmas usually meant dolls, dollhouses, doll clothes, dolls' accessories, dolls' cars, and many other items associated with the color pink. Around Christmas of 1980, Wendy and Katie were to each find a "Crying Carissa" baby doll under the tree from the Big Guy. When the baby is turned on, it cries until a bottle is stuck in its sweet little mouth. We discovered around midnight that one of the cutie-pies would not cry when turned on. We double-checked the batteries that were not included. This meant taking the baby out to Santa's repair storage room where the tools were lined up on a four-by-eight piece of Peg-Board. The only way to repair the small metal contacts that were opened and closed by the action of the bottle was to gently remove Carissa's head with a screwdriver. The metal contacts were reshaped and working within ten minutes. It took an additional twenty minutes of head wrestling to get things back together. In the course of a headlock, the contacts no longer worked. Start over. The third time was indeed the charm, and Carissa was finally crying as advertised with a loud "Waaaah, waaaah."

Much sooner than later, the girls came into the den Christmas morning in their pajamas and with their hair sticking out in odd places. Wendy picked up her baby, turned it on, loved it, and put the bottle into the mouth. It was just what she had wanted. Katie picked up her (repaired) baby, turned it on, and little Carissa began her loud "Waaaah, waaah." Katie immediately dropped the doll and began holding her ears while shouting "Make it stop, make it stop!" She really did not know that I, indeed, could make it stop. Where was my screwdriver?

There is a tree placed inside our house every Christmas. I know there is some lovely tradition about bringing the family together on Christmas Eve, popping corn on the open fire, stringing the popcorn, placing brightly colored ribbon onto the tree, and opening the one present given to each person. We still bring in a tree. But often, it is right after Thanksgiving, and it may be an artificial tree because trees that have been cut down are no longer "live trees" and will be extremely dry and brittle before anyone has sung the "Twelve Days of Christmas." The stores are in full swing for Christmas shopping by Columbus Day. I really enjoy the Christmas season, but it does seem that we have created quite a gap between the early traditions and the modern ten-week forced march.

I visited Mother in early December of 1981, and she asked if I would help decorate her tree. She said that my sister was supposed to come over and help but, so far, had not made it. The great tree was still wrapped in the mesh provided by the tree farm. Mother had walked around and selected her own tree and had one of the workers cut it down and tied it onto her car. Most of the people who work on such tree farms obviously have never put one of their trees into a metal tree stand because there is never enough length left on the tree trunk to properly fit into the stand. A few of the lower limbs must always be trimmed to make that work. Mother's tree had two limbs remaining at the bottom, very near the edge where the tree had been cut down. Unfortunately, these two limbs grew upward on each side of the tree over half the total height. Now I had big gaps in a tree that Mother said looked perfectly shaped when she picked it out. I cut the limbs and shaved the ends to a point so they would fit into holes I drilled into the main trunk of the tree. The remanufactured limbs were then wired to the limbs above so the weight of the lights and decorations would not pull them out, causing them fall to the floor. I warned Mother not to move the tree or lean any presents against it because the tree could very well fall completely apart. A few weeks later, when we visited for the family gathering, I was amazed to see the tree still standing. As we left, I told my sister that she could take the tree down and to please try to have it done in time for the Super Bowl. The next year, Mother bought an artificial tree, and I don't believe she ever visited the tree farm again.

Most of us realize the joy of giving. Receiving a gift is also very pleasant, even if the tie won't match a thing in the closet or you are a medium size and the sweater is an extra large. We often buy gifts because we assume it really is the thought that counts. On occasion, we find something we really want to give to someone and hope they, in turn, will really like it. We did give our eleven-year-old cousin Phil a gift one Christmas, and he exclaimed, "Oh boy, *another* Scout Knife!" Not the response we were searching for. Still, it may be better than the Sunday school parties where boys are asked to bring a boy-gift and the girls a girl-gift. By the time the party is over, someone is unhappy and really wished they could have taken home what they had brought as a gift in the first place.

At our family gathering, there is a children's multiplication storybook that is unwrapped and rewrapped every Christmas and given to some unsuspecting family member. This tradition happened by accident when the gift label got on the wrong package, and no one could remember who was supposed to get the book anyway. The book simply began an annual journey of bouncing from family member to family member. We could always count on a spouse who was new to the family getting the book and doing their dead-leveled best to act like they really liked it.

One year, Jerry had talked too much about Indian arrowheads he had found on some property he owned and how they were special and he was always looking for new finds. At Christmas, we built a glass case and placed in it anything we could find that vaguely resembled the shape of an arrowhead, including sticks, seashells, and pine bark. We then labeled each piece as if it had some great Indian historical significance. More than once, one of the guys received an electric fork that was simply a plastic-handled, two-pronged grilling fork with an electric cord glued into the handle. We had to keep a close watch on a couple of folks to make sure they did not try to plug the thing into a wall socket.

Finally, what would Christmas be without the pageantry of the season? We can find Santa and the elves at the mall, concerts in the churches, live Nativity scenes, festive light displays, concerts, and carolers. I believe that I have participated in some type of Christmas music presentation every year since my first days in the choir at Hilton Terrace Baptist Church in 1963. I thought John W. Peterson was the only person who wrote Christmas cantatas in those days because that is all we ever sang in the small Baptist churches I attended.

When we lived in Marietta, Lynda and I always enjoyed going to Ms. Jo Evelyn's house just before Christmas to go caroling in the neighborhood. We made a special effort to go by some of the local residents who might not be able to get out of their homes to enjoy the season. With flashlights and song sheets, we would gather in the front yard as a member of the group would knock on the door (most often, Ms. Jo would give them some advanced warning that we might drop by). The short concert always ended with "We Wish You a Merry Christmas." Afterward, we returned to Ms. Jo's home and would stand near the fireplace as we drank hot cider, ate decorated cookies, and visited with fellow carolers. We always went home feeling as if we had done something that might have connected us to a deeper spirit of the season.

Merry Christmas.

THE GREEN PUMPKIN

There is substantial research successfully proving a positive correlation between one's personality and the type of automobile that person chooses to drive. We can easily identify a macho man in a giant truck with oversized tires or a large colorful sedan with brilliant lights glowing underneath, hydraulic systems raising and lowering the car as it travels down the street. Many young ladies seem to like smaller two-door sporty cars or convertibles, helping to define their overall cuteness, which may be required to match an image for acceptance in society.

We may wonder what goes on in the minds of those who don't care at all about how their car looks as long as the engine starts and gets them from home to the store and back. While this might indicate a conservative cost-conscious individual, others send up flares of caution when their cars are littered with their "stuff." We are left only to wonder what in the world could it possibly look like on the inside of their homes. Our uncle Roy was an accountant who firmly believed you should buy an inexpensive car that had to be driven seven years in order to get your money's worth. His cars were notoriously ugly the day he drove them off the lot, and they should have been pushed over a cliff after three years, much less seven.

Americans often experience a bonding with their automobiles and go to extremes to make sure the car they drive matches their real or imagined place in life. I think my brothers and sister provided a good example of a cross section of American drivers because each has a different individual automobile characteristic corresponding to a national grouping.

Jerry usually has a neutral-colored gas-efficient, *Consumer Reports*—recommended and short-term financed car. He even coached an early '70s green Vega wagon over eighty thousand miles, which may be a record for a car that started burning oil as it was driven off the new car lot. He also can become rather engrossed in discovering older, used cars with low miles at a sale price, always from another individual who has placed a Wal-Mart parking lot For Sale sign in the window. He says he needs another car but only keeps them long enough for a neighbor, family member, or friend to step into a predetermined profit margin and drive the car away.

Jim always had cars that paralleled his current lifestyle and priorities. Early on, he had to have a big engine, four speed, and wheels spinning like a rocket ship. During his near-hippie era, he had a VW bus and a brush-painted Dodge Dart. Now, in his later years, he only drives what he believes to be the most mechanically sound, technologically advanced VWs he can find. That's because, by his own account, *he* is the most mechanically minded, technologically gifted sibling in the bunch. He may be, but we allow plenty of room for error and avoid direct challenges.

I'm not sure whether Thom ever noticed what kind of car he was driving until after he turned fifty. For many years, an automobile served only as a transport for musical instruments and equipment to the next gig. There were many nights when traveling required sleeping in the car. Once, after loading his car, he backed over a four-thousand-dollar acoustical guitar that somehow had not found its way into the trunk. He played a lot of music, worked here and there, but spoke little of the mysterious musical tour he was on for about twenty years. Today, he is choosy about his ride, has a respectable job, and owns his own home.

Dede's early cars were sporty two-door vehicles that helped maintain her aura of a cheerleader, college student, and eventually, bank employee. By the time she reached high school age, the four brothers had all moved on, leaving her with the opportunity to have a new car, go to the "in" high school, and have her tuition paid while in college. She really worked on her image when she bought an MGB sports car. When it was running, it was really cute. But, alas, several bumpy relationships and three children later, any car that will start and get her to work seems to be the right image for now.

It would be a good idea if this section moved on to another topic, but my family would publish disclaimers and file suit if I didn't mention a couple of my own automobile preferences. I like cars and trucks and have owned several. I began to wonder how many vehicles have I had over the years.

I started in 1964 with a hand-me-down 1952 Plymouth. My brother Jim had originally purchased the car, had it painted green, drove it as fast as it would go, damaged the front end, sold it, and moved on. My father decided that the car needed to stay in the family and returned to the lot where my brother had traded and bought it back for fifty dollars. I was sixteen and should have known a fifty-dollar automobile might not be a great car. The Plymouth was a two-door Cranbrook—a six-cylinder straight shift green car with no front grill. The keys to the *Green Pumpkin* were handed to me between my junior and senior year in high school. Every time I bought gas, I added a quart of oil. And that is how I got started.

If you consider all the cars I have purchased, including those that my wife and I have purchased along with those we bought for our three daughters, the grand total is currently up to a total of forty-eight automobiles over a period of forty-four years (see exhibit A). I was seriously hoping for a lower average of one a year, but the math does not work in my favor. I may have been personally responsible for formulating the automobile financing term *of being upside down*, meaning that the amount you still owe on the car is more than the value of the vehicle. I am sure that I have lost more money trading cars as a result of "upsidedownedness" than the amount Jerry has spent on all his cars, the Vega not included.

If each of my siblings represented one area of the general auto-buying population, I have tried to represent the entire driving nation. There were six all-terrain 4x4s, six pickups, and a Corvette for the macho side. Three convertibles were added to project the right image. There were several mild-mannered four-cylinder engine sedans intended to save on gas. In order to keep up with the Joneses, we purchased two Lincolns, a Lexus, and four SUVs. There were several classic lemons: a1960 Ford Falcon I traded to Jim for a home-built stereo; a world famous 1978 AMC Pacer station wagon that Lynda and Alexis loved when it was not in the shop; a first-year model 1986 Ford Aerostar van that was memorable when all five of us were crammed into the cab of a tow truck as the van was hauled for a forty-mile ride at 2 a.m. on a fun-filled vacation; a lemon yellow 1968 Opel station wagon that had an oil leak and bent an engine rod within the first five thousand miles; and finally, a 1974 Pinto wagon that was worn out by forty thousand miles.

Of the forty-seven total, there were twenty-four that were purchased new. Our three daughters each got new cars on their sixteenth birthday and were each advised of the most significant driving rule: *No two cars should occupy the same space at the same time*. All three girls broke the rule. Katie and Alexis have broken the rule more than once. Wendy tested the rule but only bent it a couple of times. She did provide several driving challenges, and a car afforded her more independence than we really ever wanted to know about. Wendy called me just months after getting her car and wanted to drive to the beach with a group of cheerleaders. She assured me that there were two other cars with parents driving who were accompanying the group. She went on to describe how they would travel in a caravan, and the car would remain parked during the weeklong stay. I yielded to her solid appeal for driver safety. The deal fell apart when she received a ticket for running through a red light on the first night of the trip, returning from a teen club at 1:00 a.m. Although she promised to pay the fine, the fifty bucks did not make up for the episode.

Within two weeks of getting her new car, Katie was driving alongside Wendy, who was driving her boyfriend's car. Katie swerved, over steered, and ran into the boyfriend's car then caromed into the median and plowed several hundred feet before stopping. Everyone was OK, but the police officer and insurance agent were very curious about why sisters were running into each other. I was interested as well but never found out details of the events leading to the accident. Katie's car was repaired and served her well through high school, college, and into her first job. The accident did make it difficult at times to get the driver's door open. She had to climb out the car window wearing her new business suit on the first day of her new job at an upscale Buckhead mall. While climbing in and out of her car would make the *The Dukes of Hazard* fans proud, it ended with her first post college paycheck and a visit to a Honda dealer.

On a couple of occasions, Alexis effectively employed her car's front bumper and grill to open the trunk of the cars that had stopped in front of her. Although generally a safe driver, Alexis had her memorable automobile moments. She once got out of her Jeep in our driveway without setting the brake or leaving the shifter in gear. The vehicle started rolling backward, knocking her down, and leaving a tire tread mark on her side and leg. The Jeep continued to roll across the cul-de-sac and into a neighbor's front yard. More than a little lucky to have only minor injuries, she limped into the house to call Mom but first had to deal with a phone call from angry neighbor because the Jeep was in her yard on their grass. The incident was very scary at the time, but fortunately, we can now look back and consider that Alexis was our only child who almost ran over herself.

We have driven everything from the Green Pumpkin to a Lexus. Our girls have had new cars when they completed driver's education and passed their driver's exam. Each girl had to sign a notarized contract before getting the keys (see exhibit B). But our entire family is aware of the good fortune we have experienced when we read this. Each of us has broken the "no two cars" rule and looking back, shaking our head with wonder, but grateful for the finding laughter in the memories.

Exhibit A

Cars I Have Known

Year	Model	Comment
on or about		
1952	Plymouth	Green Pumpkin; 1st Car
1965	Simca	Rear engine
1966	Dodge Dart	Two-door hardtop
1956	Ford F-150	Junk truck for paper route
1961	Ford Falcon	Junkier, traded it for a stereo
1969	Opel Wagon	Lemon yellow—for good reason
1971	Ford Five Hundred	Good, solid transportation
1954	Ford sedan	Classic ride to W. GA
1967	Blue VW	Everyone had one, rebuilt the engine
1974	Pinto Wagon	Bought new; worn out at 80K
1966	Dodge Dart	Another 225 cu. in slant-6
1971	Toyota Land Cruiser	Best 4x4 of all
1979	Chevy 1500 PU	Good truck
1980	Pontiac Bonneville	Big family car
1982	Ford Courier	Single-again mobile
1978	Jeep CJ-5	Hardtop, no air
1979	AMC Pacer	Love/Hate relationship
1983	Jeep CJ-5	Ragtop
1984	Pontiac Bonneville	Pacer had to go
1986	Ford Aerostar	Big, roomy, a real lemon
1985	Jeep Wrangler	Red ragtop w/ air
1986	Nissan PU	Great little truck
1988	Mazda 323	Daughter #1
1988	Volvo sedan	Anything over the Aerostar van

1989	Chevy PU 454	Rocket truck
1991	Mazda 929	Smooth riding
1990	Toyota Tercel	Daughter #2
1993	Miata	Cute
1995	Toyota Avalon	Nice, cost efficient, boring
1994	Jeep CJ	Daughter #3
1996	Ford F-150	Basic and manly
1998	Ford PU 4x4	Black bad ride
1997	Lincoln Town Car	Cool
1997	Lincoln Town Car	Cooler
2000	Toyota PU	Tiny red ride
2001	Toyota Camry	Save on gas, practical
1996	Isuzu Trooper	Daughter #3 (again)
2002	Ford Explorer	Bumpy
2003	GMC PU 4x4	Diesel
2004	GMC Envoy	Leather and with cup holders
2004	GMC PU 4x4	Gas cheaper than diesel
1994	Corvette	Looked great in the garage
2004	VW Bug Convert.	Beach bug
2006	GMC Yukon	Roomy w/ cup holders
2006	GMC PU 4x4	Back to diesel
2008	Miata	Back to cute
2007	Yukon XL	Big to bigger
2005	Lexus 430	Bells, whistles

EXHIBIT B

Date _____
CONTRACTUAL AGREEMENT
BY and BETWEEN
The Parents: Party 1 and Party 2
Hereafter referred to as **PARTIES**
With their daughter(s)
Wendy, Katie and Alexis
Hereafter referred to as **DAUGHTER**

As a result of *DAUGHTER* attaining the age of 16 years; and upon properly securing a valid Georgia Driver's License; and having expressed the desire to undertake the responsibilities of automobile ownership; the following duties and stipulations are set forth and hereby established upon signature by *DAUGHTER* and both *PARTIES* named above.

Section 1.

Both *PARTIES* jointly agree to provide necessary financial support; assist in proper preparation of driving techniques; assist in instruction for proper maintenance and care; and other responsibilities as set forth below:

A. Party 1 bears direct responsibility for assuring appropriate auto insurance coverage; will provide for necessary negotiation with *DAUGHTER* in frequency and destination decisions related to vehicle operation; and will provide direction to *DAUGHTER* to assure the strict enforcement of this contractual agreement.

B. Party 2 bears direct responsibility for assuring that financial obligation for full payment of vehicle is met in accordance with a standard contract with a selected financial institution; will participate in negotiation and enforcement of the contractual agreement as necessary.

C. Absolutely no other single driver under the age of 25

PAGE TWO

DAUGHTER—Contract, continued

Section 2.

With acceptance of the keys to the vehicle, *DAUGHTER* does hereby agree to the strict adherence of the following stipulations:

A. *DAUGHTER* will wear her seat belt at all times that the vehicle is in operation.

B. *DAUGHTER* will never operate the vehicle while under the influence of alcohol or other controlled substances.

C. Absolutely no other single driver under the age of 25 shall operate the vehicle unless accompanied or specifically pre-approved by one or both *PARTIES*. This is both a requirement of the *PARTIES* and for insurance and safety purposes.

D. *DAUGHTER* will never purposefully abuse the vehicle through excessive speed; nor make any attempt to "show-off" for her peers; nor ever attempt to operate the vehicle in a manner which would not allow her full concentration on the responsibilities of driving, i.e., excessively loud radio, too many occupants in the vehicle, romantic expression.

E. *DAUGHTER* will respect the final and absolute decision of her mother (Party 1) in determining proper use, destination, and frequency of use of the vehicle. *DAUGHTER* agrees that the decisions of both *PARTIES* dictate the privilege of owning a car and will attempt to understand that disagreement over the use of the vehicle is solely based on the *PARTIES'* love for *DAUGHTER* and concern for *DAUGHTER* general health and safety.

F. *DAUGHTER* will assure the proper maintenance of the vehicle through frequent checking of the oil and other routine checks. This will include becoming completely familiar with the service and operator's manuals and becoming proficient in routine care which includes maintaining a clean appearance inside and out, as well as knowing how to change a flat tire.

G. *DAUGHTER* bears the direct responsibility for earning adequate funds necessary to buy gas for the vehicle. There should be no expectation that either of the *PARTIES* can incur any additional expense for usual operational costs.

PAGE 3

DAUGHTER—**Contract, continued**

H. *DAUGHTER* shall maintain an overall "B" average in school work. This stipulation is preferred by both *PARTIES* and, more importantly, is considered as a financial responsibility of *DAUGHTER* for purposes of reducing insurance rates.

J. *DAUGHTER* shall enroll in a driver's education class during the first available opportunity as a further measure to reduce insurance rates.

Section 3. Consequences

A. Based on initial agreement and provided that all stipulations contained herein are met, the vehicle will be considered by both *PARTIES* to be, in effect, owned and operated by *DAUGHTER*. *DAUGHTER* will have the right to make responsible decisions about the vehicle and will be able to proclaim that it is, in fact, her car. However, should any one of the above stipulations set forth in Section 2 not be strictly adhered to, the following will result:

1. Minor infractions will result in the keys to the vehicle being taken away and use of the vehicle terminated for a period of time solely determined by one or both *PARTIES*. Once such termination decision is made, it shall be final and non-negotiable.

2. Repeated infractions or major infractions will result in the vehicle being impounded away from *DAUGHTER'S* residence for a period of time solely determined by both *PARTIES*.

3. Any major abuse or disregard for the stipulations contained herein can result in the vehicle being permanently removed from possession of *DAUGHTER*

Section 4. Signatures.

The signatures of *DAUGHTER* and *PARTIES* below indicate that this agreement to uphold all specified agreements, stipulations, and rights contained herein.

_____

(DAUGHTER)

_____

(PARENT)

_____

(PARENT)

Sworn to and subscribed before me this ____ day of _____,
_____

SEAL _____

Notary Public

MAH-NA MAH-NA

Communication with infants and toddlers can be quite entertaining, especially while observing an otherwise reasonable adult interacting with such a tiny person. Most social exchanges are governed by common rules of courtesy, and among adults, one should never sweetly say, "Hey, sweet baby," in a high-pitched voice over and over while less than eight inches from the other adult's face. Grown-up exchanges should also avoid blowing air out of the mouth to make the lips vibrate while at the same time emitting a shrill noise, resulting in the kind of sound you might hear from someone climbing out of a frozen lake, having just fallen through the ice. But with babies, this behavior is acceptable and often preferred, particularly if the strange behavior makes a child smile or, better yet, actually laugh, or giggle.

Adult behavior resulting in making children laugh may be one of life's great treats. Laughter has certainly been rewarding in our home with three daughters and now with six grandchildren, who, fortunately, do not live with us in our home. Once a child discovers one of those funny things you do, they become relentless and requesting that it be repeated until you say, "Stop!" And quickly, the laughter can turn to pouting or even crying. Playing peek-a-boo is the first unending game to be played, soon followed by riding horsey on the knee, and finally moving up to holding the child by the arms and spinning them around like a ride at the fair.

Playing with the children is usually a repeat of things each of us learned when we were small. I think Aunt Mary showed us how to lace our fingers together then demonstrate, "Here's the church, here's the steeple, open it up and look at the people." Uncle Doug also taught us many different jokes and songs he learned while overseas in the Army Air Forces, most of which I did not teach our girls. He did share a little poem that has been delightful over the years because young children can quickly discover laughter in its absurdity:

> *One bright day in the middle of the night;*
> *These two dead boys had a fight;*
> *Back to back they faced the other,*
> *Drew their swords and shot each other.*

> *A deaf policeman heard the noise,*
> *And came to see the two dead boys;*
> *If you don't believe my story is true,*
> *Just ask the blind man.*
> *He saw it too!*

Most of the songs and poems were passed down well before children's learning channels flooded the television. As the songs and poems moved from one generation to the next, many of the words and punch lines were altered along the way. One of the most entertaining tunes we used with all our girls has been relatively unchanged through the years. In 1969, "Meh-Na Meh-Na" appeared on *The Ed Sullivan Show*, *Sesame Street*, and *The Muppet Show*. The original *Mah-Na Meh-Na* accompanied by the Snowths can still be found today on a *Muppet* recording; it can be blogged and be seen on video.

To entertain the children, I simply used my hands to form a couple of duck bill movements. The right hand "sang" meh-na meh-na, while the left hand responded dit-di, da-dit-it; left, meh-na meh-na; right, dit-dit-it-do; and so on and so forth. We made all types of variations of the tune with a child on one knee singing the first part and a sister on the other responding, placing socks on our hands and singing, having the fork start and the spoon respond—forever and ever, amen.

As the children grew older, we expanded into more complex learning songs to be performed at the table following the meal. Although my father told us that we could not sing at the table, singing there was expected at our house. As noted earlier, the words I recalled were not always the same as those others remember. Such is the great challenge of *There's a Hole in the Bottom of the Sea*. It may be altered each time it is sung as long the children understand the drill. The last phrase is built on the previous 7 or so. It begins as follows:

There's a hole in the bottom of the sea.
There's a hole in the bottom of the sea.
There's a hole, there's a hole, there's a hole in the bottom of the sea.

Then we add the following:

There's a log in the hole in the bottom of the sea.
There's a log in the hole in the bottom of the sea.
There's a hole, there's a hole, there's a hole in the bottom of the sea.

We kept adding by building one verse at a time until the last verse:

There's a speck on the flea on the wart on the frog on the knot
on the log in the hole
In the bottom of the sea.
(Repeat)
There's a hole, there's a hole, there's a hole in the bottom of the sea.

What an appropriate learning tool to prepare children for the "Twelve Days of Christmas." Around our house, the challenge of memory was always fun, and the girls all learned some version of "My Hands on My Head," which began as follows:

With my hands on my head, what is this here?
This is my hat checker, Mommy my dear.
Hat checker, nicky, nicky, nicky noo.
That's what I learned in my school.

This was also a building song where our girls pointed to a strangely named body part then add something each verse, including eye blinker, ear flopper, nose blower, meal pusher, chin whisker, bread basket, etc., until all parts were labeled and accounted for. One of my granddaughters has already been taught the preschool Internet version and corrected Granddaddy when my label did not favorably compare with hers. It really doesn't matter, for the learning song focuses on repetition, memory, and basic body parts.

As the children grew older, they had an opportunity to increase their level of participation in home-based songs and poem performances. One of our many favorites is "Bill Grogan's Goat," which I learned from my college roommate. It is a classic fun song for everyone, whereby the leader first sings a line and the audience repeats the same line, replicating the same tune. All our girls joined in early on during the family entertainment sessions.

> *Bill Grogan's goat*
> *Was feeling fine,*
> *Ate three red shirts*
> *Right off the line.*
>
> *Bill took a stick,*
> *Gave him a whack,*
> *And tied him to*
> *A railroad track.*
>
> *The whistle blew,*
> *The train drew nigh.*
> *Bill Grogan's goat*
> *Was doomed to die.*
>
> *He gave three coughs*
> *Of awful pain.*
> *Coughed up the shirts*
> *And flagged the train.*

Sooner or later, during these little artistic displays, we would move into poems and tongue twisters. The simple versions were those challenging our late elementary to middle school-aged kids to "say these three lines quickly, without stopping!" It never failed to produce a laugh. It was especially funny for first timers who took it on thinking it was a Peter Piper scheme. Here, you say these three lines without stopping:

> *The Smart Fellows*
>
> *There was one smart fellow and he felt smart.*
> *There were two smart fellows and they felt smart.*
> *There were three smart fellows and they felt smart.*

There were many variations on the theme, some involving barnyard animals that will be skipped, but the one listed above stayed with us for years. Now past the midway point into her thirties at the time of this writing, we are still able to bait Wendy into trying. She might get through the first line but never seems to get past the second round before we all burst out with laughter.

During the nineteen years I was a church youth director, there were many challenges to provide some type of entertainment to keep the teenagers occupied. We wrote skits, songs, and poems and even put on a couple '70s versions of *Saturday Night Live*. Most of the deacons and the preacher never stayed up that late, so they weren't offended when we patterned after a sometimes risqué television show.

It was during the early 1970s in Gatlinburg, Tennessee, I was in the crowd for a summer evening performance of a country band. It was an open-air rustic stage that seemed perfect for the mixture of country music being played. The performance included a set of humorous music and audience banter, including one of the band members who alternately stomped and clapped in rhythm as he entertained us with a poem called "Them Moose Goosers." I'm not sure if anyone laughed more than I did and was struck by the uniqueness of the verse and the delivery. It was only recently that I discovered a book of "Them" poems written by Mason Williams published in 2000, but obviously written years earlier.

Them Moose Goosers

How about Them Moose Goosers,
Ain't they recluse?
Up in the boondocks,
Goosin' Them Moose.

Goosin' them huge moose,
Goosin' them tiny,
Goosin them meadow-moose,
In they hiney.

Look at Them Moose Goosers,
Ain't they dumb?
Some use an umbrella,
Some use a thumb.

Them obtuse Moose Goosers,
Sneakin' through the woods,
Pokin' them snoozy moose,
In they goods.

How to be a Moose Gooser?
It'll turn ye Puce.
Gitchy gooser loose and
Rouse a drowsy moose!

When I first heard the poem, there was no published version I could find, but the poem stayed with me, and it was only natural for me to write and perform my own version at a church Valentine dinner. My first effort was to highlight a Valentine theme appropriate for a church crowd. The following poem was delivered, stopping and clapping included.

Them Lip-Lockers

Look at them lip-lockers
Ain't they grand?
One is woman
And the other is a man.

You better watch this pair
This woman and a man
'Cause they'll lock they's lips
Whenever they can.

At home, in a car
Or even at the Church
Leave by themselves and
They lips will make a lurch.

Some of these folks
Are like you and me
When they lock they's lips
They throw away the key.

Wanta' be Lip Lock?
Stick your finger in a socket
Grab you some lips
Hold on and lock it.

There are probably six or seven of these homemade poems written and placed in a folder on a shelf somewhere. My poems are only original in text. I have to give Mr. Williams and an unknown band member credit for the imaginative idea and unique presentation.

I felt the need to add one final poem. This idea is much more recent and jumped out at me following an annual elementary school recitation contest. I heard onstage presentations by children in kindergarten through fifth grade as they delivered their poems in the competition. Later the same day, two things continued to surface in my thoughts. First, I was reminded that I had also competed in a recitation contest when I was in the fourth grade. The verse was a monologue portraying two cowboys planning to shoot it out but, in the end, agreed to go have a glass of buttermilk. I did not win or place in the competition, but it was definitely a step above playing Mercury in the school play, running as fast as I could around the sun with little wings glued to my shoes and hat. Second, I could envision a six or seven-year-old reciting a poem on the stage about a little boy anxious to read a new adventure on a box of cereal each morning.

Mr. O

I like it when I wake up or when my mother yells "Let's Go!"
Because I know my time is coming to sit with Mr. O.

I hunt for clean blue jeans, pull a sock over my toes,
My hair is sort of fuzzy, but that's no problem for Mr. O.

Down the hall into the kitchen, my sister's already there,
I tug her hair as I go by and slide into my chair.

And then I get to be there, in my own little space,
I sit quietly at the table and turn my freckled face.

With a bowl and spoon before me, the sun begins to glow,
A great big box of cereal, my favorite, Mr. O

The box has Mr. O's picture, he's a hero to boys like me,
He has a shining helmet, a laser sword across his knee.

And now's the part I like the best, I turn the box around,
And read Mr. O's next adventure, the crunch of O flakes the only
sound.

In just a few short minutes, I have to rush and go,
But now I stare and read aloud as the bad guys give in to O.

I tell my mother "Thank you" then I wink at Mr. O,
He knows I'll be back in the morning, before I have to go.

You may find it funny, my mother says it's so,
But breakfast is always special with the amazing Mr. O.

I gave the poem to the coordinator of the recitation contest so the poem could be shared should a student want to use it in the competition. I was informed that all the pieces selected for competition had to have been published before it could be used. Now it has.

THE WHEELS ON THE BUS
GO ROUND AND ROUND

As a teacher and school administrator for thirty-seven years, I usually learned something different almost every day about our society. It was an education for me right along with the children who were learning to read and performing math calculations. Many of those experiences were absolutely delightful, for many times not only did the students provide rewards, but so did many of the other adults in the field of education who were supportive, friendly, and shared a common aspiration for helping children. By comparison, some of the behaviors of students and adults did have us pause to wonder, *What the heck could they be thinking?*

School administrators routinely dealt with unhappy parents. My years as a manager of special education programs, human resources, and as a school superintendent gave substance to the supposition that the truth is always stranger than fiction. We would often comment about the impact of the coming cycle of a full moon, for we knew that complaints and strange behavior would increase for about ten days during each phase. My own theory developed after considering that massive amounts of water are displaced during the daily high and low tides around the earth. It was more significant along the shores under a full moon. Since our human bodies are almost all water, a full moon would displace the water around the brain and suck the common sense out of many parents, students, and others. During the waxing of the moon, what might normally be a small emotional bump in the road might very well become an event marked by

"Then if you aren't going to change your decision, you will soon be hearing from my lawyer!"

Some of the most interesting tales come from actual bumps in the road made by school transportation employees. Please forgive me in advance for highlighting a single group in this story. The majority of bus drivers and transportation employees are some of the most reasonable and patient people I have ever met. But over the years, there are a few recorded instances where reasonable people would not have acted in such unreasonable ways.

As a newly appointed school superintendent in a small school district, I tried to get to know as many employees and to become familiar with as many of the programs as I could. We were about to begin a new school year in the system, and since it was my first school year opening as superintendent, I determined to check every aspect of our operations. One of my last stops was the school bus maintenance shop. I envisioned a beehive of activity as our crew worked to ready our fleet of thirty buses for the new school year. When I arrived, I asked the director of transportation to step out into the parking lot with me and tell me about what was going on. He was somewhat unenthusiastic about going out in the August heat with the new guy but left his air-conditioned office anyway. The bus shop had three large bays for bus maintenance. Bay number 1 was empty. The second bay had a refrigerator standing in the middle of the work area. Behind door number 3 was an automobile on jack stands and was the subject of brake job. I kept my cool as I ask about the situation. Can all the buses be completely ready for the road and not a single bus needs repair or maintenance? The director answered yes. I became somewhat more direct when I asked about the refrigerator. He provided that he was not sure. Finally, the heat got to me as well, and I said, "And why the hell is a private automobile getting a brake job in our bus shop?" With a sly grin he answered, "That is the school board chairman's car." While it took me about fourteen months to fully rectify the bus shop situation, on that day, I paused, knowing I had lost round one and said, "Well, let's get it fixed and get it out of there."

Modern technology arrived to the fleet of buses when video cameras were added to visually capture the behavior of students should they misbehave. Many times, they were helpful when a school administrator was able to visually demonstrate to a parent how unruly their child had been. Unfortunately, there were many instances where unruly behavior was not limited to a couple of boys swapping punches but an indication of a larger problem when a bus driver lacked control over the riders. Several times, we discovered that, in order to roll through the tape to get to a single action of a particular child, we had to observe six other improper behaviors by other children on our way. We also were enlightened by a driver's behavior as a result of a live camera on board. The cameras were mounted in the front of the bus, and the drivers were required to place a new tape in the recorder every day before the day's route. There were several Oscar-winning performances provided by employees who seemed oblivious to the rolling camera, which they had actually inserted a tape into the machine.

One afternoon, one of the drivers of an elementary school route called in sick within a few minutes of dismissal time. It was not unusual for someone from the bus shop to quickly fill in, and on this day, one of the mechanics, Cecil, had to go and fill in. Cecil simply climbed in and started the bus and drove to the nearby school. He probably did not think about the tape already loaded that automatically began recording with the turn of the key. As captured on the video, things did not start out very well. As the bus sat parked while loading children in grades kindergarten through fifth grade, some were loudly talking, standing, or walking around. Cecil eventually got them to sit down as he drove away from the school. Within one-half mile of the trip, he yelled, "You kids need to shut up 'cause I have a terrible headache and ain't going to put up with it!" The chatter died momentarily, but the noise level quickly rose again. Once again, Cecil advised his riders, "OK, that's it. If you don't get quiet, I'm going to stop this bus and get off."

Well, it seemed that the gauntlet had been taken up by the children who immediately started snickering and laughing. The video clearly showed the children, but we couldn't see Cecil. But the bus slowed, pulled to the side of the road, and stopped. At that moment, it seemed that every child's head was drawn by some magnetic power in a choreographed turning motion as they watched the driver leave the bus, walk along the side, and finally move past the end of the bus, and he kept walking. There was a brief pause marked by complete silence. It was the quiet before the storm. The thirty-three young children began to respond in about three distinct patterns. The first group consisted of several boys who determined that unsupervised meant that it was OK to act without restraint and began throwing things, punching other students whom they disliked, and did other behaviors forbidden by the bus book of order. Group 2 quickly decided that to stay on the bus was at their own peril, and they grabbed their book bags and headed toward the door. A couple of older girls assumed the Heisman Trophy pose and employed a stiff arm to move people out of their way as needed to get them and a younger sibling off the bus. Finally, group 3 was those children who were torn between personal safety and school rules. This generally younger group began to cry.

Fortunately for school officials, the bus was no farther than two miles from where it started the afternoon route. Also, a parent and a school grounds maintenance man stopped to see if the bus driver needed help. Finding no driver, they called the school and began to herd the children back into the bus. The school principal and transportation director arrived in a few minutes and restored order. Four children, however, got a ride home from an individual who stopped when she saw children walking down the road. A giant liability bullet was dodged when we were able to verify that they had arrived home safely, and all were accounted for. Cecil's headache was much worse than he thought. When he left the bus, he walked to a business about a block away and called the bus shop to say he just couldn't drive because of the noise, and they would have to send over someone else. That was Cecil's last day working for the school system.

Sometimes, unusual behaviors are discovered through a more unusual series of events. In this instance, the coordinator of special services received a call from a parent of a special needs child. The mother wanted to know if the smaller school bus designed for disabled students had a new driver on the route. The coordinator told her that she did not know about a change and maybe it was a substitute driver for the day. Later, when she was speaking with the transportation director about another matter, she happened to mention the question she got about special bus number 15-88. The director stated that he did not think there was a sub that day, but he would check. The director pulled the tape for the day and played it to see why the confusion. He then came directly to my office with the video.

As we began to watch, I didn't notice anything out of the ordinary. There were only two children on the smaller bus, and it was bouncing along the road as expected. Because of the way the cameras are mounted, we could not see the driver but could see all the seats behind the driver's area. Then I realized that the person seated on the front seat of the bus was, in fact, the driver. She sat with hands folded on her lap, enjoying the ride. The sound on the video clip then clearly picked up the question, "Momma, is this where we turn?" The new driver was the fifteen-year-old son of the woman assigned to drive the bus.

It did not take long to have the actual driver appear in my office, and I asked one question, "Mrs. Summers, did you let your son drive your school bus?" She replied, "Yes." I requested her bus keys and advised her that she was immediately terminated. I really wanted to tell her that she might want to call Cecil and find out what employment might still be available after such a foolhardy episode. Maybe she thought that her son's automobile learner's permit allowed for him to learn driving a bus as well.

I never checked to see if these incidents happened during a full moon, for there was no doubt that all common sense had been sucked from the brains of both drivers. I continue to hope that we never get to see those images on the *World's Funniest Videos* or live from the CNN Center.

"HOW'S YOUR MOMMA?"

There are several effective ways to deal with a company's employees and customers while improving management skills along the way. During my years in school administration, I had many opportunities for professional growth through conferences and training sessions in an effort to become proficient in dealing with personnel and parents. I tried to sort through many philosophical approaches that might best fit my own administrative style. I was able to develop a list of important things to remember along the road to success as a manager and, later, as CEO of a school district. While the list has been modified over time, there were about ten things I tried to keep in mind. I maintained a list limited to ten because most groups I worked with were familiar with a society that places everything imaginable into a "top ten" list of one topic or another.

Al's top ten leadership items are as follows:

1. *Never be five minutes late for a meeting.*
2. *Dress like you just might be the person in charge.*
3. *Reaching consensus means making everyone a little bit unhappy.*
4. *Speak directly to the person who needs to improve.*
5. *Never send a memo addressed to everyone in reaction to one person's blunder.*
6. *Ask people about their momma.*
7. *Hire the smartest people you can find.*

8. *Don't mess with people's money.*
9. *Volunteer outside of the office.*
10. *If an employee threatens to turn in their keys, take them.*

These leadership topics are best served in another book dedicated to improving the skills of future managers. Each item requires about two chapters in describing and implementing a skill. For government work, each topic might require three chapters and a corresponding set of regulations. All these issues come into better focus with experience. Asking people about their momma earned a permanent place on my list after years of high-level caretaking for our mother. Mother was very independent; and for almost ten years after her retirement, she traveled with friends, walked every day, visited her five children and grandchildren regularly, shopped, and had more hobbies than she had time. Each of us had to immediately rethink her independence when she had a stroke at the age of seventy-four.

All five children initially pitched in following her first stroke in 1995, and we took turns staying at her apartment, helping her make the transition from independence to a significant limitation in her mobility. She had a second milder stroke the next year that seemed to transfix her with a permanent physical limitation, and it also deflated Mother's initial goal for regaining her freedom. She had a short-lived burst of hope for recovery following a hip replacement in 1997. The follow-up physical therapy was encouraging and had Mother speaking of walking at her apartment complex around the swimming pool area, and she even imagined being able to drive again. But she had so many other related aliments that she eventually had to accept her confinement. Over the course of the next nine years, my oldest brother, Jerry, and I maintained a regular routine of care and support and kept the other siblings updated on her progress. As we began to share the stories of her last years, I discovered many experiences that were uplifting during a time that otherwise might have provided the entire family with a steady dose of depression.

The beginning months following her stroke, she continued to move about the house with the aid of a cane and used a walker when we went out. She still maintained a low level of independence and wanted to know when we would let her drive her car again. I agreed to take her to a local mall to shop for items she insisted that she needed, and I was not capable of selecting the correct products she had in mind. She directed me to drive to an area that was nearest the entrance of a large department store. At the yellow curb, with a lot of assistance, Mother got out and began with her walker to make for the front door. I told her to wait on the bench in the foyer while I parked the car. I quickly parked and came in to assist with the shopping spree. Mother had not waited. I began to make a slow circle around the merchandise counters, trying to determine which direction she had taken. By the time I made the third round, I thought, *Great, I have lost my mother on our first venture.* How in the world could she have gotten away from me in only four minutes while I was parking the car? Although the store was crowded, I finally located her in the ladies' undergarment department, which explained a lot about my own inability to shop for her.

During those years of physical disability, Mother continued to maintain a positive outlook as best she could. She also maintained a positive attitude toward eating. When she was able, we took her to some of her favorite restaurants. One of the first times Jerry and I offered to go out for lunch, Mother insisted that we go to the new Chef Lee Chinese Restaurant. The new place was very ornate with a colorful façade and an entrance designed with a glass floor over a large pool of live gold fish. We loaded Mother and her walker into the car, along with her neighbor who was capable of loading herself, and off we went. Mother provided directions. That turned out to be a problem. We made several "I think we turn here" maneuvers, and we continued, led by her encouragement that it was just a little bit farther. When we crossed the county line north of the city, we determined that, unless we were traveling to mainland China for a meal, we needed to do some serious backtracking. We stopped twice to get new directions and arrived at our lunch destination, where Mother informed us that if we had not missed a turn, we could have found it much sooner.

While the Chinese restaurant was a favorite of hers, she often preferred an eatery where everything but the sweet tea was fried. We traveled to exotic places like Ezell's Catfish Cabin with vegetables and fried food, Rose Hill Seafood with potatoes and more fried fish, and Kentucky Fried Chicken for her favorite—a large chicken potpie. When went to pick up a meal to-go, we often would place the bag in the back of the truck rather than to smell the fish on the way back to Mother's apartment or to have a greasy stain on the floorboard carpet. It was not our intent to hasten Mother's poor health toward an artery-clogged end. Such trips for these foods were limited to once or twice a month. For most of the time, she only had simple meals cooked or heated in the microwave at home.

In February of 2003, we decided to have a special lunch outing in honor of Mother's eightieth birthday. Mother's sister, Betty Ann, drove in to join us for the occasion, and it was no surprise when Mother announced that she would love to go to Chef Lee Chinese Restaurant. Every journey was now a wheelchair trip: roll out to the car, stand up, drop down, and load the chair in the trunk. Our aunt's Cadillac was the car of choice. Things worked out very well, and we eventually made it back to her apartment. Jerry and I were feeling pretty much full of ourselves over the successful special occasion and expressed our hope that Mother had enjoyed her birthday. She responded, "It was very nice. I couldn't have asked for a better seventy-ninth party." It was at that point that the discussion began. We reminded her that it was eighty years. She replied that we were dead wrong, and she was seventy-nine years old, and of course, she knew how old she was. The line in the sand began to deepen when Jerry began a search for Mother's birth certificate. We were not going down without a fight. Although it took a while, Jerry produced a document claiming that Mother was born in 1923 and was, in fact, eighty years old. Mother finally conceded with "Well, I guess I am eighty. But that birth certificate may be wrong." Her independence remained intact.

Our greatest asset during these years of confinement to the apartment was the discovery of Miss Queenie. This lady was perfect for the job requiring light cleaning and preparing simple meals. The physical maneuvering of Mother was left up to Mother and her canes and walker because Queenie was in her late sixties and could offer little direct lifting. But Mother had someone there with her every day, and during the first few years, she also drove Mother to the doctor, dentist, and grocery store. Later, Mother had to have stronger assistance for mobility.

Jerry and I determined that Mother had to have a power lift easy chair. We eventually found a medical supply company in town that was very familiar with the process for senior citizens assistance, which was new territory for us. A young lady named Gloria, with a very short dress, was quite helpful and took care of acquiring the necessary doctor's report and forms for Medicare assistance needed for the big chair, which she would have delivered to Mother's apartment at no charge. We quickly deemed the recliner as the "electric chair." It was surprising how many times we needed to visit the store and discuss with Gloria other physical assistance apparatuses for Mother. Each of us accused the other of having an interest in what Gloria might be wearing when we visited, rather than a concern over a specially designed walker that would offer Mother more stability. More accurately, the taunting was comic relief between brothers that was necessary to aid in getting through some of the more difficult times.

My brother and I developed a standard routine to travel to Mother's every few weeks and check on things. Jerry would balance the checkbook, review the bills, and make bank deposits for the few checks that came in each month. I usually gathered all the medication to determined what needed to be reordered, but more importantly, I would count the number of pills in each of the bottles in an effort to discover if Mother was taking her medicine as prescribed. We tried the weekly pillbox tray when all she had to do was to open the "Wednesday lunch" section, for example, and wash them down. She wouldn't use it and insisted that she could remember. We insisted that she couldn't. We were right, but she was stubborn and we got to a point of hoping for about a 65 percent success rate. Taking medicine was similar to getting Mother to wear the medical alert button around her neck. We established a calling account, as seen on TV, for her after about the third fall when Queenie couldn't lift her off the floor. Not long after the purchase of the medical alert, we discovered an ugly bruise on her face during our visit. We asked about the medical alert, and Mother told us that it bothered her when she slept so she would hang it on the bedpost at night. That was where it was found the morning she fell and hit her face on the nightstand. For a while, she at least wore it during our visits (we think Queenie reminded her when we were coming), but we had little guarantee that it was swinging around her neck otherwise.

One morning, we had prepared breakfast for Mother and were going about our routine chores. I went into the bathroom to wash up and took out my tiny blue hearing aid and laid it on the counter to keep it from getting wet. I left to change shirts and got involved in a discussion about a financial issue and did not go back to retrieve the hearing aid until later but could not find it. I began a search through my bag, shaving kit, dresser, and soon expanded the search to other rooms, but it could not be located. Frustrated, I asked Mother if she had been in the bathroom and had seen the little hearing aid. She said she had been there but had not seen anything. After a long pause, she said, "I did see a bug on the floor, but I wrapped in toilet paper and threw in the trash can." I had a slight gasp for breath just before she said "trash can." I was certain she was about to let me know that a two-thousand-dollar bug had been flushed down the toilet. Sure enough, I found a small rolled-up ball of toilet paper in the trash can containing the hearing aid. I later thought that it actually looked like a bug and decided that clearly I was the one who needed to be more careful.

Mother's former independent life of many activities in her church, traveling with friends, and taking on new hobbies slowly began to narrow to the confines of her apartment. Her world became a list of medications, doctor's appointments, and discussion of the next meal. It was always a brief shock to our system as we ventured into her changed world from our own busy schedules. To simply walk out the front door into the parking lot of her apartment may as well have been a journey into a foreign country for Mother. She preferred old TV reruns of *The Andy Griffith Show* in Mayberry over modern sitcoms. She would often fall asleep in the electric chair with the Braves playing baseball. Miss Queenie would come and go along with occasional friends or neighbors. The 650 square feet of her apartment became her confines.

There were several instances when we enthusiastically sought alternatives for her living arrangements. We began with discussions for assistive living. She finally agreed to consider a nice place similar to where two of her close Sunday school class friends lived. We visited there, as well as three or four large assistive care facilities. We also visited smaller homes that had been converted for assistance for four to six women. We finally located a nice larger residence that we thought she would like and that we all could afford. We called the siblings and discussed it. We also knew that she needed to move ahead into such a facility because she was on the borderline for the physical independence required for minimum levels of assistance. We sat down with Mother to share the colorful brochures, had the blessing from even the most reluctant youngest brother, and had a date scheduled for a visit to meet the intake official and staff. I felt like I was trying to sell ice to Eskimos. Finally, Mother leaned back in the electric chair and replied, "I ain't going to no damn nursing home!" We knew there was no room for negotiation, for as much as we wanted her to routinely have competent staff support, she honestly would not have been able to remain for very long before she, indeed, had to move to a higher level of required care—a nursing home.

Maintaining the higher level of care in her apartment continued to work as well as we could make it. Home Health care came three times a week, Queenie worked every weekday, neighbors were checking in as they could, and all the children were keeping up with her status. Eventually, the only way to transport Mother was by wheelchair. Doctor appointments were assisted through community transportation with a lift on the van. A trip to the bathroom was similar to watching a slow motion replay of syrup dripping from the bottle on a winter day.

In one of our visits, we were following the routine of checks, medicine, and food. I sat near Mother and told her again we were concerned about her being alone at night and the potential falls. I also mentioned that based on her physical condition, only a nursing home would be able to meet her needs. She then said, "I'll go to a nursing home." I sat still simply looking at her, somewhat in disbelief. I finally replied, "Now, Mother, I'm talking about a nursing home, not an assistive living center." She said that she understood, so I kept moving and told her that the best nursing home facility we knew about was one hundred miles away in my hometown of Jackson. Without hesitating, she agreed to go to Jackson.

This turn of events was quite a shock to Jerry and I who knew this day would come, but had not assumed that Mother would respond with such a matter-of-fact approach. Making the many arrangements for a bed, termination of the lease, etc., took about two months. In January of 2004, we loaded the now famous electric chair, Mother's antique dresser, a small rocking chair, and her clothes to her new room at the nursing home. Since it was located in our hometown, Lynda or I could check on her daily. Jerry and Cindy were only an hour away and came regularly to visit and provide support. On her eighty-first birthday, we gathered all five children and as many grandchildren as we could muster and celebrated the occasion at our home. Looking back on it now, it was almost as if Mother had called a meeting of her children, counted heads, looked us over, and decided that each of us were doing about as well as could be expected. That was the last family gathering with our wonderful matriarch at the center of our attention and in charge.

The next few weeks at the nursing home took a quick turn. Her appetite dwindled; she remained in her bed all day and communicated only when we directed a question to her. I came into her room one morning wearing a dark suit, and Mother made a comment that I was a little dressier than normal. I replied that I had been to a funeral of a local resident. Without further comment, she said, "I want Brother Kevin to conduct my funeral. I'd like my Sunday school class to serve as honorary pallbearers. The grandchildren could serve as pallbearers." By the time she got to the pallbearers, I had grabbed a napkin and was taking notes. This was an important moment because Mother had never openly discussed death or dying. She added some scripture to be read and two songs to be played. As casually as I could, I asked a few questions to be sure that I had the correct information. I took the napkin home for safekeeping.

Shortly after that, she was transferred to the hospital next door because she did not eat and was often comatose. In the hospital, we spoke with her only once when she responded to our questions. Eventually, the family decision was made not to feed by tube, and she was moved back to the nursing home room and made as comfortable as possible. She passed away a few days later with the family at her bedside. As she literally took her last breath, I have always remembered Jerry's final words: "Goodbye, Mother."

The extended transformation of Mother's memorable independence through several stages to total dependence is not unusual or different from many families who have experienced similar emotions of having to care for a parent. Lynda and I shared many comparable times with her mother and father before they passed away. Around our dinner table, our family recalls our parents and grandparents for the vibrant and personable individuals they were during the fullest extent of their lives. We want our children to hear the stories and understand how we found strength and humor in otherwise depressing situations. For each person who may read this, please find a calming reassurance when you must say, "Goodbye, Mother."

I'LL FLY AWAY

Johnny is a good friend and neighbor who is also quite an adventuresome fellow. He runs his own business, loves to snow ski, and is a licensed instrument-rated pilot who has flown regularly for over twenty years. He owns a six-passenger, single-engine airplane located at a hangar on a grass strip four miles from his home. While discussing one of his more recent interests, I discovered that he was taking courses at a sailing school out of Amelia Island, Florida—one of our favorite vacation destinations. Sailing seemed like such a wonderful idea, so I decided to go with him on the next trip to take the beginner's course while he spent the weekend in a level 3 overnight training. We flew from the grass strip for a two-hour flight to the Fernandina Beach Municipal Airport. The sailing school instructor picked us up at the airport, and we headed for the harbor. Johnny grabbed his bag and climbed onboard his boat for a three-day onboard lesson, and I went to the beginner's class for hopeful sailors. Saturday was filled with "this is a boat" curriculum, including basic knot-tying and man overboard drills. Sunday was a mix of classroom time, sailing in the bay, and followed by a required paper-pencil test for certification. Johnny and I met back together on Sunday afternoon to fly home and returned through low clouds and rain, finally breaking through into the sunlight at about seven thousand feet. We talked about sailing and flying during the entire trip home.

Several days later, I saw Johnny, and he wanted to know if I enjoyed sailing. I replied that while I certainly enjoyed the sailing, I discovered that I was very interested in flying, and we began a discussion of flight school possibilities in our area. After my wife, Lynda, and I considered that learning to fly for a fifty-four-year-old might be similar to that of teaching an old dog a new trick, she encouraged me to give it a try. I persevered, and in August of 2001, I enrolled in a small flight school in Macon, Georgia, at the old city airport.

When I showed up for my first lesson, I did notice that most of the students and all the instructors were a lot younger than I. Most of these men and women were hopeful of becoming commercial pilots and needed to log many hours of flying necessary to meet the minimum requirements. Flight instruction provided them with a means to that end. I also discovered that many of the students and most of the instructors were from India and Pakistan. However, my first instructor was a young American male who always seemed to be wearing large aviator glasses while working to project an aura of coolness. I never called him Fonze to his face, but the image was almost too real to pass up.

So it was the Fonze who took me out to an airplane for my first lesson. As is typical of beginning flight, we walked over to a Cessna 152, a two-seater airplane. I was directed to get in on the left or the pilot's side. This was my first surprise, for I thought surely he would fly me around and explain the basics of the plane. This was the beginning of many experiences that really made it more difficult for this old dog simply because it was much harder for me to let go of years of learned behavior. Of course, I immediately began to steer the plane with what looked to be a perfectly good steering wheel. When taxing around the airport while on the ground, an airplane's direction is controlled by foot pedals. I quickly came to understand the basics of an airplane through direct confrontation between what my brain was telling me and what the airplane actually had in mind.

We spent the first few hours practicing takeoffs and landings and learning the formal protocol for runway patterns and approaches. Two days following my third lesson, all flight instruction ceased as a result of September 11, 2001. I could only wonder what I had gotten into because the media photographs of the terrorists looked very similar to the people in the hallways around the flight school. The individuals who flew directly into buildings in New York learned their skills through small flight schools. Most schools remained shut down for several weeks, and I did not resume lessons for one month. Fortunately, our instructors were only responsible for high anxiety among the students. No bad guys located in Macon.

After about six or seven more lessons, the Fonze decided that he needed to move on to other things, and he resigned from the flight school. My new instructor was from Pakistan with an accent that required me to ask him to repeat his instructions about forty times before I began to distinguish a different rhythm and emphasis in his speech pattern. He also looked very much like the pictures in the paper from a month before.

The new instructor, Priyacant, along with his wife, Mandeep, was a part of a husband-and-wife team who both were flight instructors at the school. I hoped that they had adopted American first names like Sam, Chip, or Jane, but these two stuck with their given names brought over from Pakistan. It took a while for me to get the names correct. Since I was older than their combined ages, they were comfortable calling me Mr. Alan, which usually sounded a bit more like "Meester Allen," as in "Meester Allen, get the wing up. Meester Allen, you are off-line. Meester Allen do not bounce the plane," etc. It was especially intense when following instructions for practicing in-flight stalls. We practiced these maneuvers almost every flight and literally placed the plane in such an attitude that the air no longer supported the wings, and the plane "stalled" and became a rock instead of an airplane. What fun. A similar gay old time was practicing flying at the slowest speed possible while maintaining altitude and remaining on course. I slowly began to learn new tricks.

After about fifteen hours of flying instruction, Priyacant had me go through several takeoffs and landings, coming to a full stop and taxing back to the runway for takeoff. He instructed me to come to a stop on the entry ramp in the middle of the field and said, "Meester Allen, can you do what we just did three times in a row?" I told him I saw no problem with repeating the maneuvers, at which point he said, "Good." He unplugged his headset, opened the door, got out of the plane, and began walking back toward the flight building. It took a few moments for me process the impact of his instructions, but I decided not to think about it and started to move toward the runway and to begin the three takeoff and landing cycles. But more importantly, this was my first solo flight. Lynda had often said that she wanted to know when I was going to fly solo. As it worked out, my report to her was by phone on the way home after I had completed the flight and had given up my shirt, so the instructors and other pilots could sign it for display to commemorate the occasion.

During the next few months, we practiced various maneuvers again and again. Flights became more complex, including visits to other airports, night flights, and cross-country excursions—both with an instructor and as solo. Every flight with an instructor included engine-out drills when the power was cut back and the student had to determine an emergency landing in a field, on a road, or on an alternate runway if available. This was a surreal practice because I learned procedures that I really could not quite imagine happening during an actual flight although I knew such experiences took place every day. One of our students and his instructor were unsuccessful in making an emergency landing within a mile of the runway and perished in a wooded area. However, the statistics for safety were definitely on our side for airplane travel, and almost all of us returned to flight within a few days after the memorial services for our fellow pilots.

Mandeep took over as my flight instructor for the remaining one-third of my training. I am unsure of the details of Priyacant's grounding, but the Federal Aviation Administration (FAA) had a host of rules that resulted in questions about some record keeping and other matters unknown by me. But Mandeep was an excellent instructor who was determined to get this old guy through the process. It was her drill and practice both in the air and in the flight school classroom that helped pave the way to course completion. In August of 2002, I passed the flight test and became a licensed private pilot. It came just one week shy of a full year and a total of seventy hours of flying time since I had started.

So now what? It made sense to me that if I had a pilot's license, I needed an airplane. I discovered an aircraft dealer located at a small airport in South Georgia where we began negotiations on an affordable airplane. I soon discovered that affordable meant one thing to me and another to every airplane owner in the state. But we finally settled on a 1974 Beechcraft Sport, a 150-horsepower plane only flown by a little old lady to church on Sundays, and it was downhill both ways. Or so it seemed. But it was a very reliable small plane with ample room for two along with a small seat in the back for one other adult if we only filled the fuel tanks halfway. Because this was a low-winged plane compared to the high-winged Cessna, I enlisted Mandeep to go with me and to provide the required flying time for a different type of plane. She also had to sign off on takeoffs and landings at the grass field where we were to hangar the plane. This tactic was especially interesting since most pilots had only one choice, regardless of the wind direction, for entry to and exit from the short grass field because of the surrounding tall pine trees.

One of my first cross-country trips in our plane was to travel down to the Georgia coast, have lunch, and return. Johnny agreed to accompany me for the two and one-half-hour flight each way. One of the many FAA regulations requires flight plans to be filed before takeoff and closed upon arrival at your destination airport. This process also allows the pilot to speak to air traffic control along the way. They usually speak quickly using a language that saves time and is designed to often confuse new pilots in small planes. I might have heard, "One nine seven five Whiskey go to 4,000 and hold, maintain two seven zero." I determined that the first number called out was the one painted on the side of our plane and that I should try to fly a certain number of feet above the ground while headed in a specific direction. We followed our directions, landed, and walked over to a restaurant for lunch and finally headed back. Somewhat unrelated to my compulsiveness to do everything correctly while trying to enjoy the trip and the lunch, I neglected to close the flight plan on our arrival at the airport. The FAA does not like this to happen. The procedures required to wait for a specified time and then make a few calls to find out if the aircraft landed on a designated runway or if it had landed at an odd angle in the swamp before it reached the coastal island. Unfortunately for me, one of the first calls they make is to the home phone number listed in the flight plan. Just imagine the reaction when Lynda got the answering machine message from the FAA that they had not heard from N1975W. When Johnny and I made the return flight, we corrected the error, and I properly opened and closed the return plan as we landed. Correcting the message with Lynda was another matter. The air traffic controllers could not compare with the rapid fire directions I received from my wife about all future flying excursions and the proper procedures to be used for home and airport.

Lynda did begin speaking to me after only a few short months, and she continued to fly with me. We decided to upgrade our plane and get a slightly larger engine so we did not have to be as concerned about additional weight like an extra hat and jacket. The good used plane salesperson in South Georgia made a trade, and we purchase a 1983 Beechcraft Sundowner with a new engine and up to 180 horsepower. It was very similar to the first one but with a few more features. We flew that plane for over a year and had a great time. When we considered purchasing a second home in Florida, we were faced with a tough decision. We knew how great it would be to be able to fly down to the beach, but there was no way we could afford both airplane and beach house. I suppose there are many things worse than replacing a Beachcraft with a beach house, but that is what we did and my piloting days came to an end.

INDEX

A

Adult behavior, 87

agreement, 45, 60, 83, 86. *See also* contract

airplane, 109–12. *See also* takeoffs; landings

airports, 64, 71–72, 108–12

Alabama, 37

Alexis (Alan White's daughter), 5, 72, 78–79, 83

alumni association, 35–36

American Indians, 25

Ash Street Baptist, 60. *See also* music

Ash Street Youth Program, 60

aspirin, 14. *See also* Mercurochrome

automobiles, 76–78, 96. *See also* cars

B

bail bondsman, 34

Baptist churches, 54, 56, 61, 75

   Belmont, 59

   Hills Crossing, 59

   Hilton Terrace, 56–57, 75

   Raymond, 55

   Woodland Hills, 60

Baptists, 29–30, 54–57, 59–61, 75

beehive, 18, 96

behaviors, 13, 45, 49, 54, 87, 95–98

Bernice (Alan White's student), 43, 47–48

"Bill Grogan's Goat," 90

bus, 16–18, 95, 97–99

bus shop, 96–98

C

cabin, 37–40, 68, 102. *See also* trailer

Canasta, 26

cars (*see also* automobiles), 11, 18, 27–28, 30, 34, 38, 45, 51–53, 58, 60, 74, 76–79, 81, 84–85, 96, 101–3

catfish, 37, 39, 102

Cecil (bus mechanic), 97–98